prayer

prayer

exploring a great spiritual practice

Richard W. Chilson

John Kirvan, series editor

SORIN BOOKS  Notre Dame, Indiana

www.sorinbooks.com

ISBN-10 1-893732-97-5

ISBN-13 978-1-893732-97-1

Cover and text design by Katherine Robinson

Printed and bound in the United States of America.

Library of Congress Cataloging-in-Publication Data

Chilson, Richard.
Prayer / Richard W. Chilson.
p. cm. — (Exploring a great spiritual practice)
ISBN-13: 978-1-893732-97-1 (pbk.)
ISBN-10: 1-893732-97-5 (pbk.)
1. Prayer. I. Title. II. Series.

BL560.C45 2006
204′.3—dc22

2005028517

Contents

exploring a great spiritual practice

introduction

From the unreal lead me to the Real!
From darkness lead me to the light!
From death lead me to immortality!

OM.

Brihadaranyaka Upanishad 1.3.28

We used to define ourselves as the animals who talk to one another before we discovered that other species, notably dolphins and whales, seem to do so as well. We see ourselves as the creatures that can laugh. And that may well hold since hyenas and other creatures that seem to be laughing are not really doing so. A monkey's laugh is a sign of anger and aggression, not delight. But it is apparent that humanity is the only creature that prays. The praying mantis is only adopting the posture. If anything she is preparing to eat her mate. Only people pray.

What is prayer? Well, it would be easy to say that prayer is communication, talking in plain English, to God. But Buddhists do not believe in God and they engage in prayer-like behavior—hopefully not as misleading as the mantis. Yes, Buddhists pray for healing and guidance. In Tibet the deities are aspects of enlightened beings. Each deity is capable of giving some kind of spiritual power.

So maybe we can define prayer as communication with the real. For most people that real is God, and for many people God is personal, even made flesh in human form. For others the real is the way it truly is—Nirvana, some would call it. Whatever it might be, in prayer we are stretching out our being toward something much greater than ourselves.

God wants us to understand prayer.
First, we must know through whom and how our prayer begins;
so he told me: I am the foundation.
Second, he wishes to teach us how to pray best:
our will should be conformed joyfully to God's will.
Third, he desires us to know the fruit and outcome of our prayer:
to be united and similar to our Lord in all things.
God intends our prayer and trust to be magnanimous.
If we do not trust as much as we pray we do not honor God fully,
and we place obstacles in our path.
This happens because we do not realize that
God himself is the ground of our praying.
Our very ability to pray is a gift of his loving grace.
We cannot ask for mercy and grace
unless they have first been extended to us.
Sometimes it seems after praying a long time
we have received no answer.
Do not let this get us down.
God simply wishes we should wait for a more suitable time,
or more grace, or a better gift.

Julian of Norwich

Who Is Praying?

Let us begin with a consideration of just what we want from this book. You have some interest in prayer. But who are you? Who is this that desires to pray? This book can be a guide to a very personal journey—an excursion exploring the phenomenon of prayer.

So at the beginning take some time to ask yourself who you are as a "pray-er"—a person who prays. When did you first learn how to pray? Did you say prayers as a child? Did you learn to pray before you went to bed? At family meals?

What was your experience of prayer? Did you feel comfortable praying? Did you pray alone or with your family? Did your family take part in religious services? Did they celebrate religious feasts at home such as Passover or Easter?

What was your experience of prayer as a young adult? Did you cease participating in religious services? Did you lose your faith in God? Did you find a new faith? Did you continue to pray? Did you pray regularly? Did you learn different ways of praying? How was your prayer different from your prayer as a child?

Who are you now as a person of prayer? Does your belief in God or your

Every man **prays** in his own language, and there is no language that God does not understand.

Duke Ellington

religion differ as an adult? Do you have a prayer practice? When and where do you pray? Do you pray alone? With others? Are you connected to a religious tradition? Do you participate in public worship? Who are your mentors in the spiritual life? What or who has had the greatest impact on your prayer life?

Do you have a prayer community? Do you feel the need and the use for such a group? If you have a community, how does or can that communal prayer ground and support your own project of building a prayer life?

As you journey through this book explore the many ways of praying we shall encounter here. There are many prayers gathered here—some may be from your own spiritual tradition, some not. Try on each of the prayers. Pray them more than once. By passing over into these various ways of praying we will broaden our own understanding of prayer and we will return to our own tradition the richer for the journey.

Who Do We Pray With?

Our individualist society naturally regards prayer as a solitary activity. But it is not so throughout the spiritual world. Traditionally individual prayer is approached from within the context of a wider community of prayer. For example, the Christian would pray primarily in church. Then his or her personal prayer would flow out of and into that larger world. The Jew prays first in the context of the

community of the synagogue and the family which supports individual prayer. The Muslim may pray in solitude but he or she is joining with the worldwide community by honoring the sacred times for prayer.

The prayer community not only provides a society for prayer but a tradition of prayer. How do I pray? Who am I praying to? What do I pray? Do you really want to try to pray while ignoring thousands of years of wisdom from your people on what prayer is? In this book we can briefly consider some of the many aspects of prayer but that does not substitute for what the depth of one tradition can provide.

Although prayer might be a natural human activity, especially when we find ourselves threatened, it is also something we are taught. Our first teachers are our parents and our childhood religion. As adults we find teachers who promise to make us pray-ers. We may call them gurus, spiritual directors, or companions. They occupy an important place in our modern spiritual communities.

exploring a great spiritual practice

chapterone

The God of Prayer

The God of Our Understanding

Perhaps you already have a relationship with God. You grew up within a religious tradition or you embraced a new religion or spirituality as a young adult. The understanding of God within that tradition should heavily influence your present journey into prayer.

What if you have difficulty relating to God? Images from your past may prohibit your belief in God. They may even lead you to think that you cannot believe in God. For you this journey through humanity's experience of God in prayer is a test to see whether you can embrace God at all.

Bill W., the founder of Alcoholics Anonymous, had just such difficulties as he sought to get sober. He was told that he had to believe in God. But he could not do so because of the baggage that the concept of God carried for him.

Then someone suggested he embrace a God of his own understanding. This act might lead to a relationship with God. In AA itself this idea developed into the concept of a Higher Power. What power can you believe in that is greater than yourself? This is enough for a start. As you continue this relationship, more can be discovered about this Higher Power.

God, I offer myself to Thee—
to build with me and to do with
me as Thou wilt.
Relieve me of the bondage of self,
that I may better do Thy will.
Take away my difficulties,
that victory over them may bear witness to
those I would help of Thy Power, Thy Love,
and Thy Way of life.
May I do Thy will always.

AA Third Step prayer

So let's begin our exploration with just this Other. That Other is the most important thing in your prayer life. This is the one with whom one is in communication. What or who is this Other for you?

The Christian theologian St. Anselm defined God as "That than which nothing greater can be thought." God is the Ultimate, The One without whom there is no other. The word

"God" itself refers to only one Reality. Most people today acknowledge that there is only one God.

Many believe all people worship the same God no matter how they name or understand God. Allah is not a different God from the Christian or Hindu God. Allah is but the Islamic name for the One God. And if people in Hinduism worship Brahma or Vishnu that does not mean that they believe in different Gods but that they find those figures best mediate for them the ultimate reality.

Some call on the Lord, "Rama," some cry, "Khuda,"

Some bow to Him as Gosain, some as Allah;

He is called the Ground of Grounds and also the Bountiful,

The Compassionate One and Gracious.

Hindus bathe in holy waters for His sake; Muslims make the pilgrimage to Mecca. The Hindus perform puja; others bow their heads in namaz.

There are those who read the Vedas and others—Christians, Jews, Muslims—who read the Semitic scriptures.

Some wear blue, some white robes,

Some call themselves Muslims, others Hindus.

Some aspire to bahishat (Muslim heaven), some to swarga (Hindu heaven).

Says Nanak, Whoever realizes the will of the Lord,

He will find out the Lord's secrets!

Adi Granth, Sikh scripture

Because God is the Higher Power and Ultimate Reality it is understandable that all attempts to define God will fall far short. Our thought and language break down as we attempt to describe the Ultimate. We enter a world of paradox.

God is at the same time totally transcendent and totally immanent. God is beyond all attempts to encompass God and at the same time closer than your breath. God is Lord of Creation and the most intimate Friend or Lover. To describe God both of these poles must be kept together in tension.

Even then God easily escapes our grasp. St. Thomas Aquinas spent most of his life writing a book gathering together the best we could know about God. One day he did not appear at his writing bench. His disciple finally found him in the chapel. He had had a mystical experience. He had met God face to face. All he could say when his disciple asked him to return to his writing was, "It is all straw." He never wrote another word.

The psychologist Rudolf Otto described God as "mysterium fascinosum et tremendum." The mystery at the same time draws us in with tremendous power, as it awes us, even frightens us, with its inscrutability.

The God Krishna manifests both aspects, as do most images of the deity. Arjuna, the warrior of the Bhagavad Gita, sees Krishna as the destroyer of worlds.

> *Arjuna saw the entire universe, divided in many ways, but standing as (all in) One (and One in all) in the body of Krishna, the God of gods. . . .*

You are licking up all the worlds with Your flaming mouths, swallowing them from all sides. Your powerful radiance is burning the entire universe, and filling it with splendor, O Krishna.

The Supreme Lord said: I am death, the mighty destroyer of the world, out to destroy. Even without your participation all the warriors standing arrayed in the opposing armies shall cease to exist.

Bhagavad Gita 11

In another image Krishna sits on the branch of a tree playing his flute. His music pleases the three mild maidens of Gokula. He dances with them in the moonlight. In the Christian tradition we have an image of God's transcendence in the giving of the law in flames on Mount Sinai. And the ultimate image of immanence is the infant Jesus asleep in the manger or held in his mother's arms.

Let us begin with the idea of a Higher Power. God is more than me. One alcoholic has said he knows only two things about God and that is enough. First, God is very, very smart. And second, God is not pissed. This could be a wonderful start.

It immediately addresses one problem many people have with God: God as angry, judgmental, or punishing. We received these images from a corrupt Christian or Jewish spirituality which made God all too human. We projected images of our weak fathers onto God. And when we make these fallible images of fatherhood infallible and infinite, we create a monster God.

The true Christian image of God is one of infinite love and forgiveness. The Good Shepherd leaves the ninety-nine sheep behind to go out in search of the one lost. And he risks his life until he finds that one that is lost.

If you struggle with an image of an angry God, allow the Good Shepherd or a similar image of God to replace any images you have of fire and brimstone. Your passage from an angry to a loving God will not happen overnight. After all, you have lived with this image for most of your life. It will take time to allow a more compassionate image to supplant it.

Early Humanity

Let's begin in the beginning. In the dawn of our race, what did we worship? Certainly the sun. And the moon. Perhaps the stars. The sea. The mountain. Each of these was a sacrament for the divine—an encounter with the divine through material form. Where do you find God in nature? Have you worshipped God in nature?

Just as the soft rains fill the streams,
pour into the rivers and join together in the oceans,
so may the power of every moment of your goodness
flow forth to awaken and heal all beings,
those here now, those gone before, those yet to come.
By the power of every moment of your goodness
may your heart's wishes be soon fulfilled
as completely shining as the bright full moon,
as magically as by a wish-fulfilling gem.
By the power of every moment of your goodness
may all dangers be averted and all disease be gone.
May no obstacle come across your way.
May you enjoy fulfillment and long life.
For all in whose heart dwells respect,
who follow the wisdom and compassion, of the Way,
may your life prosper in the four blessings
of old age, beauty, happiness, and strength.

Traditional blessing and healing chant

Our old **women gods**, we ask you! Our old women gods, we ask you! Then give us **long life** together, May we live until our frosted hair is white; May we **live** till then. **This life that now we know!**

Tewa tribe

Early peoples would have a difficult time responding to a question concerning their religion or spirituality. For them religion is part of who they are. It is not something they can adopt or put down. It is part of the essential fabric of their lives. Nor is it something for the individual. It belongs to the tribal essence.

Pagan Gods

Civilization is established and the gods change. Think of Zeus, the father of the gods. Or Wodin, his Northern counterpart. Then Hera, the queen mother of the gods. And Apollo, the god of order and harmony. Dionysus, the demigod of wine and festival. Diana, goddess of the hunt and the moon. And Venus, goddess of love.

What would it be like to worship such gods? You wouldn't take them all that seriously. These are gods, according to Homer and the other singers, who interfere in human lives for their pleasure. They use us like kick balls. They trick and lie. These are the gods of the state. The gods of our past. The gods who have brought us here. It is good to give offerings to the gods. It is so little one must do.

When Christianity entered Northern Europe it encountered the local gods. How could it help people move away from a belief in many gods so they might come to know the one God? The different gods were replaced by Christian saints. So today people can glimpse aspects of God in the lives of saints and may ask the saints to help them appreciate the different rays of divinity. St. Christopher became a patron of travelers, St. Jude oversees lost causes, and above all the Virgin Mary reveals the feminine aspects of God. These saints are not other gods. They mediate in human form the immensity and inscrutability of the true God beyond all thoughts and words.

What human being, image, or story most powerfully mediates God for you? Consider the images which have been powerful for you throughout your life. What most speaks to you of God's utter transcendence? What most speaks of God's immanence?

God the Mother

Many images of God throughout the great traditions have been masculine. Certainly the Western image of God is thoroughly so. We find more feminine images

of God in the East, but even there the dominant images are male. Many feel this is the result of patriarchy, and today people are seeking a feminine face of God. This face can be found in Hindu goddesses such as Durga or Kali and in the Buddhist symbol of compassion Kuan Yin. In the West the Virgin Mary is the dominant female figure.

Teach your children
what we have taught our children—
that the earth is our mother.
Whatever befalls the earth
befalls the sons and daughters of the earth.
If men spit upon the ground,
they spit upon themselves.
Chief Seattle

Under the guidance of feminism some today honor the Goddess. They call upon Mother Earth to help us restore the balance of nature. Some new pagans attempt to honor the Mother and Father equally.

For as surely as God is Father,
so surely is God also Mother,
Jesus is our true Mother by nature
because he has created us.

He is also our Mother by grace,
for he took our created nature upon himself.
All the lovely deeds and tender services of motherhood
may be seen in him.
The human mother suckles her child with her own milk,
but Mother Jesus nourishes us
with himself,
the priceless food of eternal life.

Julian of Norwich

But there has always been a hint of the feminine side of God even within the patriarchal traditions. The late Jewish scriptures sing of Sophia (Wisdom), God's first born in whom all things are imagined. "For wisdom, the fashioner of all things, taught me. There is in her a spirit that is intelligent, holy, unique, manifold, subtle, mobile, clear, unpolluted, distinct, invulnerable, loving the good, keen, irresistible" (Wis 7:22).

These scriptures also speak of God's Spirit—ruach—another feminine noun. Ruach becomes the Christian Holy Spirit. Feminist theologians today reclaim this Spirit as feminine. And finally Shekinah—God's presence—is

Wisdom has built her house, She says, "Come, eat of my bread and drink of the wine I have mixed. Lay aside immaturity, and live, and walk in the way of insight."

Proverbs 9:1ff

another feminine aspect. She appeared to Moses in the burning bush. And she ushers in the Sabbath. In Kabbala, Jewish mysticism, she becomes the first emanation of God.

Hinduism

When we consider the Gods of Hinduism it is hard to know where to begin. First of all is Hinduism itself. It is not really a religion in the way that Christianity or Buddhism are. Hinduism is simply the term used to cover the religions of the Indian subcontinent that are not Buddhism, Jainism, Islam, or Christianity.

There are literally thousands of Gods all the way from local tribal Gods to the great metaphysical players such as Brahma, the king of the Gods, or Kali who feasts on corpses and represents the dark side of life.

The Hindu is a not really a polytheist. Rather he or she is simply honoring the divine under a particular image. Which flash of divine splendor most touches you? God as mother? God the all devourer? The folk God Krishna seducing the milk maids? Hinduism opens its arms to the literally infinite number of experiences of the divine.

May the wind blow sweetness,
the rivers flow sweetness,
the herbs grow sweetness,

for the People of Truth!
Sweet be the night,
sweet the dawn,
sweet be earth's fragrance,
sweet be our Heaven!
May the tree afford us sweetness,
the sun shine sweetness,
our cows yield sweetness—
milk in plenty!

Rig Veda

The central triumvirate of Gods—almost equivalent to the Christian trinity—are Shiva, Vishnu, and Brahma. Brahma is the creator, Vishnu the preserver, and Shiva the destroyer. One may focus at any time upon one of these aspects but it is necessary that all of them be held in tension together.

Recently Ganesha—the elephant-headed deity and one of the most popular divinities in the Hindu pantheon—has become popular among Westerners. Ganesha is gentle and is credited with the ability to remove obstacles. He is the son of the divinities Shiva and Parvati. He was created by Parvati from the dew of her body mixed with dust.

Perhaps Ganesha is so appealing to Westerners for his gentleness. Many in the West have grown up under the threat of an angry, judgmental God. The very sight of Ganesha dispels any thoughts of vengeance.

In addition modern spiritual movements have brought Hinduism to our attention. One can approach God through being a yogi—a person who devotes himself or herself to God by practicing yoga and meditation. One can approach God through song and worship as the followers of Krishna do.

The God of the Hindu scriptures—the Upanishads—is beyond the gods represented in the various statues and pictures. Here is the God of the philosophers. The wisdom of the Upanishads (and the Bhagavad Gita) are the equal of any human attempt to understand God. The Christian theologian Raimundo Panikkar has said that they would make a far more profound basis for Christian contemplation than the God of the Greek philosopher Aristotle who undergirds much Christian theology.

The central holy word for both Hindus and Buddhists is the syllable OM. This word itself is said to be the name of the Holy. To pray it correctly brings one into the very presence of God. It opens and closes many mantras and prayers.

The goal which all the Vedas declare,
which all austerities aim at,
and which men desire
when they lead the life of continence . . .
is OM.
This syllable OM is indeed Brahman.
Whosoever knows this syllable obtains all that he desires.
This is the best support; this is the highest support.
Whosoever knows this support
is adored in the world of Brahma.

Katha Upanishad I

Buddhism

It is a little difficult talking about Buddhism and God. Buddhism is not atheistic. Indeed, certain schools of Buddhism have more deities than many religions. But these gods are not regarded in the same way as the Western God. They can not save us. They are not personal. We must find our own enlightenment.

The Buddha is not a god but an ordinary human being. The difference between him and other people is that he is truly awake. He has managed to find enlightenment for himself and through his great compassion he shows us the way. But we must make our own journey.

The Buddha says first that existence is not satisfactory. There is no real lasting happiness here in this state of being. But there is a cause of this dissatisfaction. That cause is the act of craving. Of trying to hold on to things. Of reaching out for more. Of hating. Of desiring. There is a way out of craving. There is a way to Nirvana—the way things really are. And that is the Noble Eightfold Path.

Four Noble Truths

1. Suffering exists.
2. Suffering arises from attachment to desires.
3. Suffering ceases when attachment to desire ceases.
4. Freedom from suffering is possible by practicing the Eightfold Path.

Right View	Right Livelihood
Right Thought	Right Effort
Right Speech	Right Mindfulness
Right Action	Right Contemplation

So the Buddhist sets upon the Noble Path and along the way he or she calls on the Buddha for guidance. He is the great teacher.

But eventually in Far Eastern Buddhism the Buddha came to stand for enlightenment itself. Buddhists see reality in terms of three Buddha bodies. So the Buddha body, while not the image of some God, becomes the image for the whole of reality calling us into its ever open, ever compassionate being.

Further, this truth of openness—that all is open and empty of self—is the nature of reality and so, since all reality is empty of self as is the Buddha, then all reality shares in Buddha nature. As some schools of Zen teach, we are already enlightened since we already share Buddha nature. Enlightenment is not something to attain. We already experience it. All we need do is let go of our clinging to this unreal self. So Zen can say that sitting is satori—enlightenment.

While Buddhist teaching encourages everyone to embark upon the Noble Eightfold Path, which includes a deep practice of meditation, few are willing or able to undertake such a project at this time. Most Buddhists are not monks or nuns but lay people in the world.

What about all these people? Do they have a chance at enlightenment? The Pure Land School of Buddhism developed in the Far East. This school focuses upon the Buddha Amida who wishes the salvation of all beings.

Amida has established a Pure Land where one can meditate with no distractions. If a person prays to Amida—the prayer is "Namu amida butsu"—he or she will be reborn into Amida's Pure Land where they will be able to work toward enlightenment with no distraction or obstacles.

Through the working of Great Compassion
in their hearts,
May all beings have happiness
and the causes of happiness,
May all be free from sorrow
and the causes of sorrow;
May all never be separated from the
sacred happiness, which is sorrowless;
And may all live in equanimity,
Without too much attachment
and too much aversion;
And live believing in the equality of
all that lives. Namo Amida Budda

Universal Love Aspiration

So although there may not have been a place for prayer in early Buddhism, prayer returned both as devotion to the Buddha and petition for enlightenment. These forms of Buddhism are not as well known in the West but the Pure

Land schools have ten times as many adherents in Japan as the more famous Zen schools.

Taoism

Taoism is also ambiguous with regard to God. The Tao or the Way is in many ways similar to God, but it is actually beyond God. "It is older than the concept of God" (Tao Te Ching, 4). The Tao calls us to conform ourselves to it. That is the way to holiness and happiness.

The Way is often quite different from the way of the world. Taoism is sometimes called the Water Course Way. The action of falling water upon stone seems quite harmless and ineffectual, but over time the yielding water eats away the rock.

Today in the West the martial arts are excellent ways to practice the Tao. Of all the martial arts, Tai Chi Chuan is the most spiritual. Of course many martial arts teachers are only into the physical aspects of the art. You must find a teacher for whom the spiritual is as important as the physical.

Before the universe was born
there was something in the chaos of the heavens.
It stands alone and empty,
solitary and unchanging.
It is ever present and secure.

It may be regarded as the Mother of the universe.
Because I do not know its name,
I call it the Tao.
If forced to give it a name,
I would call it 'Great.'
Because it is Great means it is everywhere.
Being everywhere means it is eternal.
Being eternal means everything returns to it.
Tao is great.
Heaven is great.
Earth is great.
Humanity is great.
Within the universe, these are the four great things.
Humanity follows the earth.
Earth follows Heaven.
Heaven follows the Tao.
The Tao follows only itself.

Tao Te Ching, 25

Judaism

The most powerful experience of God in human history arose in the Middle East. This God has given rise to three great world religions. He is YHWH and he is He, Father, Almighty, Storm Warrior, Lover, Scoundrel. YHWH is beyond all gods and yet He is as close as my breath.

The Shema

Recited four times daily: twice during the morning service, once during the evening service, and again before going to bed.

His name is not to be spoken. YHWH are the four consonants of His name. The vowels are "ah" and "yeh." He first appeared to a shepherd in the form of a burning bush. He sent this Moses back to Egypt where his people were enslaved. Moses confronted Pharaoh: "Let my people go." After many plagues the Pharaoh relented and the people fled. But Pharaoh recanted and pursued them in his chariots. The people soon found themselves at the edge of the sea. Who would save them now?

Hear O Israel, The Lord Our God, the Lord is One. Shema Ysirael, Adonai Eloheinu, Adonai Ekhad."

And lo the waters dried up and the people passed over safely. And when the soldiers pursued them into the waters the waters fell back and destroyed them.

Exodus 14

And YHWH led the people into the wilderness. There Moses went up Mount Sinai where God gave him the Law which would show the people how they should live. The center of that Law is the so-called Ten Commandments. These emphasize that you shall have no other God but God. "I saved you, brought you out of slavery and into a new land which I will give you. You shall be my people and I shall be your God."

And a stormy relationship it has been: a stable but unsatisfactory marriage. The people became a great nation, Israel. But her glory was short lived. The state was finally conquered by the Babylonians and the upper classes were dragged off into exile. Even then the dream did not die. God would once more bring His people out and restore them. And so God did through the Persian King Darius. Israel learns that no matter what is happening to her it is due to God's will and God will remain steadfast.

Prophets arise throughout the course of Israel's history. These speak God's word to Israel. They may warn Israel to amend her ways—especially the way she treats the poor. The prophet may warn of impending disaster as Jeremiah did before Israel fell. He may see a great warrior king who will restore Israel.

And throughout all her history Israel sang songs to the Lord. She sang to praise Him and his mighty deeds. She sang out in joy. She sang out in sorrow. Nothing was too little to bring to the Lord. And she left perhaps the world's most popular prayer book, which for centuries has put words into our mouths by which we talk to God.

The LORD is my shepherd, I shall not want;
he makes me lie down in green pastures.
He leads me beside still waters;
he restores my soul.
He leads me in paths of righteousness
for his name's sake.
Even though I walk through the valley
of the shadow of death, I fear no evil;
for you are with me;
your rod and your staff, they comfort me.
You prepare a table before me
in the presence of my enemies;
you anoint my head with oil,
my cup overflows.
Surely goodness and mercy
shall follow me all the days of my life;
and I shall dwell in the house of the Lord for ever.

Psalm 23

Christianity

Christianity claims that this awesome God became a human being in Jesus of Nazareth. This teacher of love was betrayed by one of his own disciples and handed over to the Roman occupiers. The Romans then tortured him and finally crucified him—an awful and cruel form of capital punishment.

But the Christians believe that Jesus rose from the dead and is going on to prepare a place for all peoples. Christians then assume a mission to bring this Good News to the world. And that Good News is that God so loves this world that God has given his own Son to redeem the world.

The full revelation of the Christian God is found in the Trinity. There is only one God. But God manifests in three persons—the Father, the Son, and the Holy Spirit. The Father exhibits the sheer transcendence of God. The Son shows us God's immanence. God takes on human flesh. And the Holy Spirit refers to the God within us—closer than our breath itself. One cannot understand the concept of the Trinity. Christians believe it is a mystery. Indeed if you feel you understand it, you are certainly wrong.

O Lord my God,
Teach my heart this day where and how to see you,
Where and how to find you.
You have made me and remade me,
And you have bestowed on me
All the good things I possess,
And still I do not know you.
I have not yet done that
For which I was made.
Teach me to seek you,
For I cannot seek you
Unless you teach me,
Or find you
Unless you show yourself to me.
Let me seek you in my desire,
Let me desire you in my seeking.
Let me find you by loving you,
Let me love you when I find you.

St. Ambrose

The mystics constitute the heart of every religion. These men and women actually experience the divine in their lives. Christian mystics developed the mysticism of love. St. Francis of Assisi finds God in all of creation, but especially in poverty and service. St. Teresa of Avila describes having her heart pierced by the lance of love. St. John of the Cross describes being ravaged by love.

Love is the underlying rhythm. And the dominant image for the Christian in love is sacred marriage, where we are married in total intimacy to God. This is the final revelation of Christianity.

Lead, Kindly Light, amid the encircling gloom
Lead Thou me on!
The night is dark, and I am far from home—
Lead Thou me on!
Keep Thou my feet; I do not ask to see
The distant scene—one step enough for me.

John Henry Cardinal Newman

Islam

Although historically Islam is the most recent world religion, it claims to be the oldest as well. Allah is not some new god but rather the God of the ages. Mohammed receives the final revelation, which communicates God's demands to humanity, namely the five pillars.

These five pillars are first the Testimony of Faith (Shahadah)—the prayer "There is no God but Allah and Mohammed is His prophet." The second pillar is the call to prayer; a Muslim prays five times a day, at sunrise, noon, midafternoon, sunset, and night. It is important that these times be exactly observed. There are guides that help the believer find the right times.

The third pillar is giving Zakat—support of the poor. There are percentages given to determine the amount of the offering. Our possessions are purified by setting aside a small portion for those in need, and, like the pruning of plants, this cutting back balances and encourages new growth.

To fulfill the fourth pillar, every Muslim fasts during the month of Ramadan. When this happens varies each year according to a lunar calendar. Ramadan occurs in the ninth and holiest month of the Islamic calendar.

Ramadan commemorates the revealing of the Qur'an to Mohammed. The fast ends with the sighting of the new moon. In addition to fasting during the day, Muslims also partake in special nightly prayers called Taraweeh. Approximately one-thirtieth of the Qur'an is recited each

The sleep of the fasting one is worship and his breath the glorification of Allah.

Rasulallah

night during these prayers so that by the end of the month, the whole of the scriptures will be recited.

Charity is an important aspect of Ramadan. While Muslims are required to be charitable throughout the year, in the month of Ramadan, it holds even more importance. It is a month to be as generous as possible and reflect on those less fortunate.

At the end of the month, Muslims celebrate a festive and joyous holiday called Eid ul-Fitr, the Festival of Breaking the Fast.

Finally each Muslim is required to make a pilgrimage to Mecca—the Holy City—once in his or her lifetime. This sacred journey (the Hajj) is a great source of renewal and conversion for many.

The Muslim calls God Allah. Allah is not His name. Allah is the name for God. Allah is the ultimate. Beyond Him there is no other. Allah is the divine sensed in every spiritual search. Beside Him there is no other. No other can be thought. Allah is beyond all our ability to imagine. Nothing can compare with Allah.

All religion comes to an end in Allah as we all find our way home. Although Islam is the last of the great religions, it also claims to be one of the oldest since it traces this revelation of the one God back to the prophet Abraham, whom Jews and Christians claim as their father in faith.

In the world there are many different roads
but the destination is the same.
There are a hundred deliberations but the result is one.

I Ching

EXERCISE

Although Islam is very insistent that there is no God but God, its prolonged meditation has produced the ninety-nine wondrous names for God. These names highlight the various aspects of God. Read through names. Spend some time with each one. How does it feel to pray it? What does it reveal about God? Which names open you to God? Which leave you neutral? Which trouble you? Spend about twenty minutes now meditating upon the names of God.

Allah.

Ar-Rahman, the Most Compassionate, the Beneficent, the Gracious.

Ar-Rahim, the Merciful.

Al-Malik, the King, the Monarch.

Al-Quddus, the Most Holy.

As-Salam, the All-Peaceful, the Bestower of Peace.

Al-Mu'min, the Granter of Security, the Giver of Peace.

Al-Muhaymin, the Protector, the Vigilant, the Controller.

Al-'Aziz, the Mighty, the Almighty, the Powerful.

Al-Jabbar, the Compeller, the Oppressor.

Al-Mutakabbir, Supreme in Greatness, the Majestic.

Al-Khaliq, the Creator, the Maker.

Al-Bari', the Maker, the Artificer.

Al-Musawwir, the Bestower of Form, the Shaper.

Al-Ghaffar, the Forgiver.

Al-Qahhar, the Subduer, the Almighty, the Dominant.

Al-Wahhab, the Bountiful Donor, the Bestower.

Ar-Razzaq, the Provider, the Sustainer.

Al-Fattah, the Opener, the Judge.

Al-'Alim, the All-Knowing, the Omniscient, the Knowledgeable.

Al-Qabid, the Withholder, the Contractor, the Restrainer, the Recipient.

Al-Basit, the Expander.

Al-Khafid, the Abaser, the Humbler.

Ar-Rafi', the Exalter, the Raiser.

Al-Mu'izz, the Bestower of Honor.

Al-Mudhill, the Humiliator, the Degrader.

The As-Sami', the All-Hearing.

Al-Basir, the All-Seeing.

Al-Hakam, the Arbitrator, the Judge, His judgment is His word.

Al-Latif, the Most Gentle, the Gracious, the "one who is kind."

Al-Khabir, the "one who knows the truth of things," the Aware.

Al-Halim, the Forbearing.

Al-'Azim, the Incomparably Great. God is indeed Great!

Al-Ghafoor, the Forgiving.

Ash-Shakur, the Appreciative, the Grateful.

Al-'Aliyy, the Most High, the Most Great.

Al-Kabir, the Most Great.

Al-Hafiz, the Preserver.

Al-Mughith, the Sustainer, the "one who has the power."

Al-Hasib, the Reckoner, the "one who gives satisfaction."

Al-Jalil, the Majestic, the Revered.

Al-Karim. God has everything, he needs nothing; therefore he can be generous.

Ar-Raqib, the Watchful, the Guardian.

Al-Mujib, the Responsive, the Responder.

Al-Wasi, the All-Encompassing, the All-Embracing.

Al-Hakim, the All-Wise.

Al-Wadud, the Affectionate, the Loving One.

Al-Majid, the Most Glorious.

Al-Ba'ith, the Resurrector, the "one who resurrects for reward and/or punishment," the Raiser from Death.

Ash-Shahid, the Witness.

Al-Haqq, the Truth, the Just, the "one who truly exists."

Al-Wakil, the Ultimate Trustee, the Disposer of Affairs.

Al-Qawiyy, the Most Strong.

Al-Matin, the Firm One, the Authoritative.

Al-Waliyy, the Protector, the Friend, the Defender.
Al-Hamid, the Praiseworthy.
Al-Muhsi, the Reckoner.
Al-Mubdi', the Originator.
Al-Mu'id, the Restorer to Life.
Al-Muhyi, the Giver of Life.
Al-Mumit, the Causer of Death.
Al-Hayy, the Ever-Living.
Al-Qayyum, the Self-Existing by whom all subsist.
Al-Wajid, the Self-Sufficient, the All-Perceiving.
Al-Majid, the Glorified.
Al-Wahid, the One.
As-Samad, the Eternally Besought, whom all creatures need.
Al-Qadir, the Omnipotent, the Able.
Al-Muqtadir, the Powerful.
Al-Muqaddim, the Expediter.
Al-Mu'akhkhir, the Delayer.
Al-Awwal, the First.
Al-Akhir, the Last.
Az-Zahir, the Manifest.
Al-Batin, the Hidden.
Al-Wali, the Governor, the Protector.
Al-Muta'ali, the Most Exalted.
Al-Barr, the Benign, the Subtle, the Source of All-Goodness.
At-Tawwab, the Granter and Acceptor of Repentance.
Al-Muntaqim, the Lord of Retribution, the Avenger.

Al-Afuww, the Pardoner.
Ar-Ra'ue, the Most Kind, the Clement.
Malik-ul-Mulk, Owner of the Kingdom.
Al-Jame', the Gatherer.
Al-Ghani, the Rich One who is Self-Sufficient.
Al-Mughni, the Enricher.
Al-Mani', the Preventer of Harm.
Ad-Darr, the Afflicter, Creator of the harmful and evil.
An-Nafi', the Benefiter, Creator of good.
An-Nur, the Light.
Al-Hadi, the Guide.
Al-Badi', the Originator of Creation.
Al-Baqi, the Everlasting.
Al-Warith, the Ultimate Inheritor.
Ar-Rashid, the Guide, the Religious Teacher.
As-Sabur, the Patient One.

Now spend some time finding your own name for God. It may be your traditional God. Perhaps now you want to reclaim the God of your childhood. What aspects of God are most important for you in your life now? Look for a name that summons God for you. What names your experience of God?

exploring a great spiritual practice

chaptertwo

The Themes of Prayer

The best place to begin our exploration of prayer is with the different subjects of prayer. What is appropriate to pray about? Truly anything you may want to say to another person is a proper subject to bring to God. You may want to compliment God, express your love for God, thank God, argue with God, ask forgiveness of God, ask God for something.

Your themes will be guided by your understanding of God. If your God is primarily transcendent you may not feel it is appropriate to be intimate. You will want to use formal language and acknowledge the distance between creature and Creator. On the other hand if your God is immanent all the language of human communication is open to you.

In our survey of the various themes of prayer (certainly not exhaustive), we will allow previous pray-ers to point the way. Pray each of these prayers. Enter into them. Pray them more than once. Let these words guide you toward your own language.

Petition

O Lord, holy Father,
creator of the universe, author of its laws,
you can bring the dead back to life,
and heal those who are sick.
We pray for our sick brother
that he may feel your hand upon him,
renewing his body and refreshing his soul.
Show to him the affection
in which you hold all your creation.

Dimma, 7th century Irish monk

When they think of prayer, most people think of the prayer of petition—prayer that asks God for something. Indeed, for many people this is the extent of their prayer, and it is a prayer that is only uttered from a point of crisis.

Jesus said, "Which of you who has a friend will go to him at midnight and say to him, `Friend, lend me three loaves; for a friend of mine has arrived on a journey, and I have nothing to set before him'; and he will answer* *from within, `Do not bother me; the door is now shut, and my children are with me in bed; I cannot get up and give you anything'? I tell you, though he will not get up and give him anything because he is his friend, yet because of his importunity he will rise and give him whatever he needs. And I tell you, Ask, and it will be given you; seek, and you will find; knock, and it will be opened to you. For every one who asks receives, and he who seeks finds, and to him who knocks it will be opened. What father among you, if his son asks for a fish, will instead of a fish give him a serpent; or if he asks for an egg, will give him a scorpion? If you then, who are evil, know how to give good gifts to your children, how much more will the heavenly Father give the Holy Spirit to those who ask him!"

Luke 11:5-13

The great pray-ers are comfortable bringing everything to God. But there is another side to this. We bring our petitions to God, but then we must let go of them. We are taught to rely upon God's will. If we are to submit to God's will, why bring these things before God to begin with? The dialogue between our wishes and God's will is a school in which we learn about ourselves and about God. We enter into an intimate relationship. This is not an easy connection. St. Teresa of Avila complained, "If this is the way you treat your friends no wonder you have so few." It is not easy, but it is astoundingly rich.

Sacrifice and Surrender

Take, Lord, and receive
all my freedom, my memory,
my intelligence and my will—
all that I have and possess.
You, Lord, have given these things to me.
I now give them back to you, Lord.
All belongs to you.
Dispose of these gifts according to your will.
I ask only for your love and your grace;
for they are enough for me.

St. Ignatius Loyola

Sacrifice has formed the core of religion from the very beginning. Humanity has always had the idea that our relation to God centered around sacrifice. In the beginning these were bloody sacrifices. But as we evolved, the sacrifice became more and more spiritual.

"What to me is the multitude of your sacrifices?"
says the LORD;
"I have had enough of burnt offerings of rams
and the fat of fed beasts;
Wash yourselves; make yourselves clean;
remove the evil of your doings from before my eyes;
cease to do evil,
learn to do good;
seek justice,
correct oppression;
defend the fatherless,
plead for the widow."

Isaiah 1:11ff

I am here **abroad,**
I am here in **need,**
I am here in **pain,**
I am here in **straits,**
I am here **alone.**
O God, aid me.

Celtic charm

So, as our spiritual insight develops, sacrifice moves from external offerings, whether bloody or not, to an interior moral sacrifice—the pure heart.

Adoration and Praise

Hallelujah. Praise God in His sanctuary;
praise God in the firmament of His power.
Praise God for His mighty acts;
praise God according to His abundant greatness.
Praise God with the blast of the horn;
praise God with the psaltery and harp.
Praise God with the timbrel and dance;
praise God with stringed instruments and the pipe.
Praise God with the loud-sounding cymbals;
praise God with the clanging cymbals.
Let every thing that hath breath praise HaShem.
Hallelujah.

Psalms 150

We offer praise and adoration to God. We praise God for God's creation, for God's goodness, for God's power. The spiritual person inhabits a world of wonder. When I am able to step back from my usual sleep and forgetfulness I become aware of the beauty, the glory of this world and this life. And my heart turns naturally to praise God.

We become aware of how the whole creation sings the praise of its creator. And even more we are opened to the mystery of the human heart. And we seek God who formed us so fearfully and wonderfully.

Most High Almighty Good Lord,
Yours are praise, glory, honor and all blessings;
To You alone! Most High, do they belong,
and no one is worthy of speaking Your Name!

Be praised, Lord, with all Your creatures,
and above all our Brother Sun,
who gives us the day by which You light our way,
and who is beautiful, radiant
and with his great splendor is a symbol to us of You,
O Most High!

And be praised, Lord,
for our Sister Moon and the Stars.
You created them in the heavens bright,
precious and beautiful!

And be praised, Lord,
for our Brother the Wind and for the air
and the clouds and for fair weather
and for all other things
through which You sustain Your creatures.

And be praised, Lord,
for our Sister Water,
so useful, and humble, and chaste!
And be praised, my Lord,
for our Brother Fire,
through whom You light up the night
and who is handsome, joyful, robust, and strong!

And be praised, my Lord,
for our Sister, Mother Earth,
who supports and carries us
and produces the diverse fruits
and colorful flowers and trees!

Praise and bless the Lord
and give thanks to Him
and serve Him with great humility!

Be praised, my Lord,
for our Sister, bodily Death
from whom no living man can escape!
Woe only to those who die in mortal sin;
but blessed are those who have done
Your most holy will;
for the second death can cause them no harm!

"Canticle of Brother Sun," St. Francis of Assisi

Thanksgiving

For this new morning and its light,
For rest and shelter of the night,
For health and food, for love and friends,
For every gift His goodness sends
We thank you, gracious Lord. Amen.

"Prayer of Gratitude for God's Gifts," Anonymous

As we awaken to the spiritual life we realize how all is a gift. Even the next breath we take is a gift when we consider it. That we exist rather than not is a gift. In the presence of this gift we feel thanks. Much prayer consists of giving thanks to God for all the gifts God has bestowed upon us. As we stir to the spiritual, we are moved to thanksgiving.

Let us rise up and be thankful,
for if we didn't learn a lot today,
at least we learned a little,
and if we didn't learn a little,
at least we didn't get sick,
and if we got sick,
at least we didn't die;
so let us all be thankful.

The Buddha

Communion

O my God, come to me,
so that You may dwell in me
and I may dwell in you.

St. John Vianney

The ultimate goal of the spiritual life is communion with the Real. This is true whether you are Christian or Buddhist. We yearn to be one with the One and with the All. We may celebrate a foretaste of that communion in a ritual like

Christian Holy Communion. And of course we will voice our desire to be one with God in our prayer.

When the signs of age begin to mark my body
(and still more when they touch my mind);
when the ill that is to diminish me or carry me off
strikes from without
or is born within me;
when the painful moment comes
in which I suddenly waken
to the fact that I am ill or growing old;
and above all at the last moment
when I feel I am losing hold of myself
and am absolutely passive in the hands
of the great unknown forces that have formed me;
in all those dark moments, O God,
grant that I may understand that it is you
(provided only my faith is strong enough)
who are painfully parting the fibers of my being
in order to penetrate to the very marrow of my substance
and bear me away within yourself.

Teilhard de Chardin

Confession and Penitence

Our Father,
forgive all our misdeeds
and wipe away our sin,
for you are great and compassionate;
your mercy knows no bounds.
My heart lies before you, O my God.
Look deep within it.
See these memories of mine,
for you are my hope.

St. Augustine

Confession has played a great part in humanity's prayer. We are limited creatures. We are bound to fall short or sin. We are caught in a world where evil abounds and we find ourselves again and again giving in to that evil.

St. Paul says that although he knows what is good, he finds himself doing evil. When this happens, we do not despair but approach God. Rather than hide or deny our sins, we confess them and are then not condemned but forgiven.

When the Stalinists set up their camps to brainwash people they found one group upon whom their efforts were vain—believing Christians. To break down a person you must find their weakness—the weakness they cannot acknowledge, the weakness they project onto others. But a real Christian acknowledges his or her shortcomings. They are confessed, not denied. So the Christian is able to see who he or she is honestly. Nothing can break him or her. They already know they are broken and yet they are loved.

For the mistakes we committed before You
under duress and willingly.
For the mistakes we committed before You
through having a hard heart.
For the mistakes we committed before You
through things we blurted out with our lips.
For the mistakes we committed before You
through harsh speech.
For the mistakes we committed before You
through wronging a friend.
For the mistakes we committed before You
by degrading parents and teachers.
For the mistakes we committed before You
by exercising power.
For the mistakes we committed before You
against those who know,
and those who do not know.
For the mistakes we committed before You
through bribery.
For the mistakes we committed before You
through denial and false promises.
For the mistakes we committed before You

through negative speech.
For the mistakes we committed before You
with food and drink.
For the mistakes we committed before You
by being arrogant.
For the mistakes we committed before You
with a strong forehead (brazenness).
For the mistakes we committed before You
in throwing off the yoke (i.e., refusing to accept responsibility).
For the mistakes we committed before You
through jealousy (lit: 'a begrudging eye').
For the mistakes we committed before You
through baseless hatred.
For the mistakes we committed before You
in extending the hand.
For the mistakes we committed before You
through confusion of the heart.

The Al Chet, Yom Kippur confession

Forgiveness

Father forgive them
for they do not know what they are doing.

Jesus from the cross for his enemies

I grant forgiveness to all living beings May all the living beings please **forgive me.** I have friendship with all **living beings.** I have **no hostility** towards anyone.

Jain prayer of forgiveness

Most religions have rituals of forgiveness centered in prayer. Jews keep a Day of Atonement—Yom Kippur—as an accompaniment to the New Year and the new life it brings. Christians put the forgiveness of sins near the heart of their faith. Orthodox and Catholics celebrate it as a sacrament. Through the sacrament the sinner is personally touched and healed by Jesus.

When Jesus taught his students about prayer and gave them the Lord's Prayer he laid special emphasis upon the command to forgive one another's sins. He said if we could not forgive, God would not forgive us.

This is not a light command. We are human beings. We all fail. We make mistakes. We do the wrong thing. And sometimes we do it deliberately. And it makes one hell of a mess. But we can ask forgiveness and make amends to one another when we hurt each other.

What are we to do? Well, almost all religions offer ways to right the wrong and allow healing to occur. It is certainly a prime theme for prayer. Do you intend to make it a part of your own prayer life? To pray to God for forgiveness? To ask for the grace to forgive others? To ask for guidance—how to approach this event in life? It is not always easy.

EXERCISE

What happens when there is someone whom you cannot forgive? They have hurt you, done you wrong, and you just cannot find the means to forgive them. In this case you might want to undertake a process to help you forgive.

Each day pray for this person's happiness. Not the happiness you want for them but that happiness they want for themselves. Do not contaminate the prayer. Keep it simple. "May John find happiness today." After a couple of weeks you should find yourself softened toward that person. You should be able to sincerely pray for their happiness.

Lament and Mourning

Thou, O HaShem, art enthroned for ever,
Thy throne is from generation to generation.
Wherefore dost Thou forget us for ever,
and forsake us so long time?
Turn Thou us unto Thee, O HaShem,
and we shall be turned; renew our days as of old.

Thou canst not have utterly rejected us,
and be exceeding wroth against us!

Prayer for Tisha B'Av, Lamentations 5:19-22

Sorrow falls into every life. Despite what some New Age trends argue, spirituality does not protect us from evil and hurt. Rather it provides a way through the pain and sorrow.

When we are hurt we will bring our lament to God. After all, God is responsible for not only the good but for evil as well. The East is better at recognizing this.

The West has tended to split evil off from God into the devil. But this does not really solve the problem because the devil is not omnipotent. Only God is all powerful. Somehow evil too is in God's hand.

The prophet Isaiah hints at this when he quotes God as saying, "I am Lord of Light and of Darkness." Furthermore, when we are at the end of our rope we almost by nature turn toward something more than us, whether we really believe in God or not. And so we bring God our lament and our grief.

Behold, O LORD, for I am in distress,
my soul is in tumult, my heart is wrung within me,
because I have been very rebellious.
In the street the sword bereaves;
in the house it is like death.
Hear how I groan;
there is none to comfort me.

All my enemies have heard of my trouble;
they are glad that thou hast done it.
Bring thou the day thou hast announced,
and let them be as I am.
Let all their evil doing come before thee;
and deal with them as thou hast dealt with me
because of all my transgressions;
for my groans are many and my heart is faint.

Lamentations 1:18-22

Complaint and Argument

Out of the depths I cry to thee, O LORD!
Lord, hear my voice!
Let thy ears be attentive to the voice of my supplications!
If thou, O LORD, shouldst mark iniquities,
Lord, who could stand?
But there is forgiveness with thee,
that thou mayest be feared.
I wait for the LORD, my soul waits,
and in his word I hope;
my soul waits for the Lord
more than watchmen for the morning,
more than watchmen for the morning.
O Israel, hope in the Lord!

For with the Lord there is steadfast love,
and with him is plenteous redemption.
And he will redeem Israel from all his iniquities.

Psalm 130

Christians have difficulty complaining to God. Jews are better able to do this. From the beginning the Jew has struggled with God. Indeed the patriarch Jacob once wrestled with God and would not give up until he had been wounded and exacted a blessing. The blessing was a new name—Israel—he who struggles against God and prevails.

In the death camps of World War II, Jews put God on trial and found God guilty. That Christians do not have this same attitude toward God is to their disadvantage.

We could see the cross as taking away anger as well as sin. Certainly Christian saints have drawn close enough to God to enter into complaint and argument.

THOU art indeed just, Lord, if I contend
With thee; but, sir, so what I plead is just.
Why do sinners' ways prosper? and why must
Disappointment all I endeavor end?
Wert thou my enemy, O thou my friend,
How wouldst thou worse, I wonder, than thou dost
Defeat, thwart me? Oh, the sots and thralls of lust
Do in spare hours more thrive than I that spend,

Sir, life upon thy cause. See, banks and brakes
Now leavèd how thick! Lacèd they are again
With fretty chervil, look, and fresh wind shakes
Them; birds build but not I build; no, but strain,
Time's eunuch, and not breed one work that wakes.
Mine, O thou lord of life, send my roots rain.

Gerard Manley Hopkins

What happens when you are deeply wounded? What happens with the anger at life's injustices? Is it not fitting to bring these emotions, too, before God? Otherwise we keep God at a distance.

Blessing

Hold on to what is good
Even if it is a handful of earth
Hold on to what you believe
Even if it is a tree that stands by itself
Hold on to what you must do
Even if it is a long way from here
Hold on to life
Even if it is easier to let go
Hold on to my hand
Even if I have gone away from you.

Pueblo blessing

May the longtime sun shine upon you, all love surround you, and the sweet light within you guide your way on.

Traditional blessing

The spiritual world is a world of blessing. In blessing we call down God's goodness on people and things. In blessing I wish you well—I encourage you to flourish.

I cannot be a spiritual person without entering into this world of blessing. I begin to turn outward to the world and to my neighbor. Their well being becomes important to me. I become more a person for others—I grow selfless. And that selflessness is expressed at least in part in the act of blessing.

The Lord bless you and keep you;

the Lord make his face to shine upon you, and be gracious to you;

the Lord lift up his countenance upon you, and give you peace.

So they shall put my name on the Israelites, and I will bless them.

High priestly blessing,
Numbers 6:24-27

Peace and Justice
Oh God, You are Peace.
From You comes Peace,
To You returns Peace.
Revive us with a salutation of Peace,
and lead us to your abode of Peace.
A saying from the Prophet,
used in daily prayer by Muslims

The Western spiritualities have been very interested in justice, particularly justice for the poor, the outcast. These themes run through the Jewish, Christian, and Muslim traditions.

For the poor and the oppressed,
for the unemployed and the destitute,
for prisoners and captives,
and for all who remember and care for them,
let us pray to the Lord.
Lord, have mercy.

"For the Poor," *Book of Common Prayer*, 1979

In the East the idea of compassion develops within the Buddhist tradition and flowers in the Bodhisattva vow that one will not enter into Nirvana until all life can join in.

And of course peace is a universal dream. It is peace that is truly the goal of every person. Peace is what one enters upon the spiritual journey to find.

In the name of Allah,
the beneficent, the merciful.
Praise be to the Lord of the
Universe who has created us and
made us into tribes and nations
That we may know each other, not that
we may despise each other.
If the enemy incline towards peace, do
thou also incline towards peace, and
trust God, for the Lord is the one that
heareth and knoweth all things.
And the servants of God,
Most gracious are those who walk on
the Earth in humility, and when we
address them, we say "PEACE."

Muslim prayer for peace

exploring a great spiritual practice

chapterthree

The Times of Prayer

Humanity has always believed that prayer is most appropriate to certain times and seasons. In this chapter let us explore the times and seasons of prayer.

Times of the Day

We begin with the times of the day. Do you have a special time of day when you pray? What might be the ideal time for you to pray? Finding this time will help you to establish a

In the beginning was God,
Today is God
Tomorrow will be God.
Who can make an
image of God?
He has no body.
He is as a word
which comes out of
your mouth.
That word! It is no more,
It is past, and still it
lives! So is God.

Bantu prayer

prayer routine. Perhaps at the beginning of the day before the kids are up? Or what about the end of the day just before you crawl into bed? Do you ride the bus or mass transit? Sometimes people find that routine appropriate for their prayer life.

Dawn

In the name of Allah, the
Beneficent, the Merciful.
Say: I seek refuge in the Lord of
the dawn,
From the evil of that which He
has created,
And from the evil of intense
darkness when it comes,
And from the evil of those who
cast evil suggestions in firm
resolutions,
And from the evil of the envier
when he envies.

Qur'an 113

Dawn is a natural time for prayer observed by almost every spiritual tradition. The natural symbol for the day is light. The world awaits a new day with its delights and challenges. All is new. All is possible. We have not yet gotten distracted by the works of our lives. Now is the time to turn to God.

You have just spent a peaceful night for which you give thanks. You look forward to a new day. What do you want to say to God? What do you want to ask of God for this day?

The Christian name for morning prayer, Lauds, means "praise." This form of prayer forms the foundation of many Protestant Sunday services, which are outgrowths of the traditional Morning Prayer.

Afternoon

Evening, and morning, and at noon will I pray,
and cry aloud and He shall hear my voice.
Psalm 55:17

Noon prayer time coincides with lunch. Both are meant to bring you back from your work. Relax. Enjoy. Talk to God.

We can get distracted in the middle of the day. A short call to prayer can bring us back to basics. Nothing too long or complex. That is more appropriate for morning or night. Just a little check-in with God. Sit back. Take a couple of deep breaths. What's going on with you?

Mid-afternoon is that lagging time of day. Time for a break. The English custom of tea is a perfect honoring of this time. Lest we get lost in our work, let us remember who we truly are and whom we truly serve.

Sunset

Lord, behold our family here assembled.
We thank you for this place in which we dwell,
for the love that unites us,
for the peace accorded to us this day,
for the hope with which we expect the morrow;
for the health, the work, the food and the bright skies
that make our lives delightful;
for our friends in all parts of the earth. Amen.

An evening family prayer

I am a sunset chaser. I love to experience that moment when the sun sinks behind the earth. Next I wait for the wonderful light to show in the clouds. Then there are the magical times when I catch the first glimpse of the new moon. And after that there is the first star.

At sunset, as we move from daylight into the shadows, our pace changes again. Work is done. We look forward to dinner and the evening. Let us give thanks for the day past and the blessings experienced.

I call upon thee, O LORD; make haste to me!
Give ear to my voice, when I call to thee!
Let my prayer be counted as incense before thee,
and the lifting up of my hands as an evening sacrifice!
Set a guard over my mouth, O Lord,
keep watch over the door of my lips!

Psalm 141

Bedtime

Now I lay me down to sleep,
I pray Thee, Lord, thy child to keep:
Thy love guard me through the night
And wake me with the morning light.
Amen.

Traditional Christian bedtime prayer

Now we approach the final change in our day—from night to sleep. The day is done; time to look back on it. Were there times I forgot myself? Did I do anyone harm? Bring all this to the Lord. Ask God's forgiveness and healing.

In Thy name, Lord, I lay me down and
in Thy name will I rise up . . . .
O God,
Thou art the first and before Thee there is nothing;
Thou art the last and after Thee there is nothing;
Thou art the outmost and above Thee there is nothing;
Thou art the inmost and below Thee there is nothing. . . .
Waken me, O God, in the hour most pleasing to Thee
and use me in the works most pleasing to Thee,
that Thou mayest bring me ever nearer to Thyself.

Attributed to Al-Ghazal

The night has always been consecrated to prayer. From time immemorial people have gotten up from their beds in the middle of the night to pray. Or they have kept Vigil and remained awake the whole night. The silence and the darkness bring us close to God.

In the Christian tradition monks and nuns got up in the middle of the night to pray Matins. This service was built around readings from scripture and the saints. The monks listened to the readings and meditated upon them.

Now that the sun has set
I sit and rest and think of you.
Give my weary body peace.
Let my legs and arms stop aching.
Let my nose stop sneezing,
Let my head stop thinking.
Let me sleep in your arms.

Dinka tribe of Sudan

EXERCISE

You might want to take a daily inventory of consciousness as part of your prayer life. This prayer exercise helps you took back at the day and bring it to God. It will take no more than ten minutes.

To begin, sit back in a comfortable chair. Close your eyes. Take a couple of deep breaths. Put your consciousness down in your feet. Feel them. Imagine them relaxing. Now move up to your lower legs. Imagine them relaxing. Continue moving up your body, imagining it relaxing. There may be parts of your body which you cannot feel. That is OK. Simply imagine you are feeling it relaxing. That is enough. Keep calm and relaxed. After you have reached the top of your head turn to the next part of the exercise.

Now review your entire day. Begin with getting up in the morning. What did you do today? Who did you meet? What were the key events? What were your dominant feelings? Do not judge yourself or anybody else. Just bring whatever is there to the Lord.

You may want to ask advice, give thanks, ask for forgiveness or healing. Let it happen. When you are done, finish with a short prayer to God—maybe asking for God's presence tomorrow, asking for guidance, or asking for help.

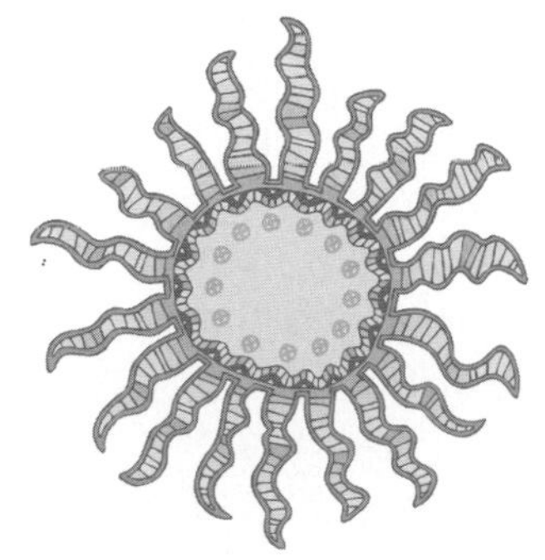

Times of the Year

Autumn

We turn from the times of the day now to the larger cycle of the year. We will enter the calendar in the fall. Fall witnesses a number of New Year celebrations, among them the Ethiopian and Korean. These celebrations are tied to the harvest festival. In ancient times people celebrated at night under the harvest moon. The moon's light also provided the opportunity to work in the fields at night.

The Autumnal Equinox, also known as Mabon or Harvest Home, is celebrated when day and night are of equal duration. It marks the beginning of the descent into increasing darkness.

Christians replaced this feast with the Feast of St. Michael and all the Angels. Michael fought and overcame Satan, so he becomes a sign that although the light is fading, it will not be utterly defeated.

The activity in nature during the summer months is slowing down, leading eventually to the hibernation of the winter. For many Pagans, fall is a time to reflect on the past season. It is also a time to recognize that the balance of the year has changed, the wheel has turned, and summer is now over.

> *We give ourselves time to stop and breathe deeply, to feel the satisfaction of what has been achieved, to start to relax.*
>
> Joint Chief of the British Druid Order Emma Restall

Fall is the time of the Jewish New Year (Rosh Hashanah) and shortly afterward the Day of Atonement (Yom Kippur). When you think about it, fall seems a more appropriate time for New Year than January 1st. In the fall students are returning to school. We have all been refreshed by our summer vacation. We are ready to start another cycle.

God is the incomparable King of The Universe.
The destiny of humanity is to come to this realization.
Whereas human kings rule
in accordance with the principle of: "might makes right,"
God is the Holy King, Who is, at the same time,
beyond comparison in His power,
"Vas er vil, Tut er"—"Whatever He wills, He can do,"
yet He is also the Father of the orphan
and the Judge of the widow,
Who is always on the side of the powerless.
He is the Incorruptible and Righteous Judge of the World,
Who favors no one, and cannot be bribed.
He is the true God and His word, the Torah, is true and eternal.

Rosh Hashanah prayer, from The Malchiyot (Kingliness) prayer in the High Holidays liturgy

The middle of autumn is given over to harvest. Christians mark it by a gathering of souls: the three feasts of Hallowe'en, All Saints, and All Souls. These feasts acknowledge and honor all beings. Like most Christian feasts, these were built upon earlier pagan festivals.

Then let us **toast**
John Barleycorn,
Each man a glass in hand;
And may his **great**
posterity
Ne'er fail in **old**
Scotland!

Traditional toast

Thanksgiving is this country's religious civic feast day. It is the only holiday that has not been changed, developed, and corrupted. We remember how the Native Americans came and shared their food with the starving Pilgrims. It is a time to gather with family and friends in prayer and feasting, giving thanks for what we have been given.

We gather together
to ask the Lord's blessing;
he chastens and hastens
his will to make known.
The wicked oppressing
now cease from distressing.
Sing praises to his name,
he forgets not his own.

Beside us to guide us,
our God with us joining,
ordaining, maintaining
his kingdom divine;
so from the beginning
the fight we were winning;
thou, Lord, wast at our side,
all glory be thine!

Winter

Winter is the time when the earth shuts down or sleeps. It is the darkest time of year and so our prayer has been a seeking of the light.

Jews celebrate the feast of Hanukkah in memory of the Temple's seven oil lamps, which miraculously burned for seven days without going out. We may be in the dark, but the light will prevail.

How wonderful, O Lord, are the works of your hands!
The heavens declare your glory
the arch of sky displays your handiwork.
In your love you have given us the power
to behold the beauty of your world
robed in all its splendor.
The sun and the stars, the valleys and hills,
the rivers and lakes all disclose your presence.
The roaring breakers of the sea tell of your awesome might;
the beasts of the field and the birds of the air
bespeak your wondrous will.
In your goodness you have made us able to hear
the music of the world. The voices of loved ones
reveal to us that you are in our midst.
A divine voice sings through all creation.

Jewish prayer for Hanukkah

Light is the concern of another feast day. Zen Buddhists celebrate December 8 as the day of the Buddha's Enlightenment. In Japan monks and nuns will prepare themselves by a long, silent retreat that emulates the Buddha's victory over illusion.

Yule means "wheel," according to one derivation. It is the Northern pagan feast of the solstice which centered around the burning of the Yule log to give light and heat in the darkest time of year.

Evergreens are used at this time of year because they are a natural symbol of rebirth and life amid winter cold and darkness. Holly was particularly prized to decorate doors, windows, and fireplaces because of its prickliness—to either ward off or snag and capture evil spirits before they could enter and harm a house.

Yuletide has been a time of peace and charity. In Norway, work had to be reduced to a minimum, and no wheels were to be turned, for that would show impatience with the great wheel in the sky, the sun. As part of this time—called Julafred, or Peace of Christmas—no kind of wildlife, neither bird, beast, nor fish is trapped, shot, or netted.

Of course the most famous winter feast is Christmas, a Christian replacement of the ancient Roman Saturnalia. All of these feasts celebrate the rebirth of the Sun as the days begin once more to grow longer.

Christmas commemorates the birth of Jesus, the Christian savior. It amalgamated into itself the cult of Mithra; December 25 was his birthday before it was celebrated by Christians as Jesus' birthday. Twelve days after Christmas, Epiphany celebrates the bursting forth of the light. This is the key feast in the Christian East.

Loving Father,

Help us remember the birth of Jesus, that we may share in the song of the angels, the gladness of the shepherds, and worship of the wise men.

Close the door of hate and open the door of love all over the world. Let kindness come with every gift and good desires with every greeting. Deliver us from evil by the blessing which Christ brings, and teach us to be merry with clear hearts.

May the Christmas morning make us happy to be Thy children, and Christmas evening bring us to our beds with grateful thoughts, forgiving and forgiven, for Jesus' sake. Amen.

"Christmas Prayer," Robert Louis Stevenson

The most recent winter feast is Kwanzaa, created in 1966 to celebrate the first fruits of the harvest. The seven candles on the kinara represent Nguzo Saba, the seven principles of Kwanzaa: Unity, Self Determination, Collective Responsibility, Co-operative Economics, Purpose, Creativity, and Faith. The

Unity Cup is poured to commemorate the family ancestors and then is shared by the family members. Kwanzaa is celebrated each year from December 26 to January 1.

Spring

For thou, O Spring! canst renovate
All that high God did first create.
Be still his arm and architect,
Rebuild the ruin, mend defect.

"May-Day," Ralph Waldo Emerson

In spring we celebrate the sowing of the new earth and the renewal of life. In early spring, the time of the monsoons, Buddhist monks and nuns retreat to their monasteries for retreat and study.

Christians observe Lent in early spring, a time to step back and examine yourself. What is your relation to God? How can you make that relationship come alive again?

Spring brings the Jewish celebration of Passover. At this time, Jews remember how God liberated their ancestors from the hands of Pharaoh. They pray for those imprisoned. They bless. They eat together. And all this takes place in the context of a sacred meal.

This is the bread of affliction which our ancestors ate in the land of Egypt.

Let all who are hungry come and eat.
Let all who are in need come and celebrate Passover.
This year we are here: Next year, in the land of Israel.
This year we are slaves: Next year may we all be free.

Prayer for Passover, traditionally spoken at Passover seder

The Christian feast of Easter builds on Passover, for Christ the Passover Lamb is sacrificed. Christ rises from the dead. As the risen Christ stayed on earth forty days after his Resurrection, so are there forty days to the Easter season.

O God, who for our redemption
gave your only-begotten Son
to the death of the cross,
and by his glorious resurrection
delivered us from the power of our enemy:
Grant us so to die daily to sin,
that we may evermore live with him
in the joy of his resurrection;
who lives and reigns now and for ever. Amen.

"The Joy of His Resurrection,"
The Book of Common Prayer

Give me a sense of humor, Give me the grace to see a joke, To get some pleasure out of life And pass it on to other folk.

"Prayer for All Fools' Day," Anonymous

On the fortieth day Jesus ascends to his Father, celebrated by Christians as Ascension Day. And the season is completed ten days later on the feast of Pentecost. It is the feast of first fruits of springtime. In Israel the feast had been called Pentecost—fifty days from sowing. It reminds Jews of the Law being given to Moses on Mount Sinai. This Law makes Israel God's chosen. For Christians Pentecost is the pouring out of the Holy Spirit upon the disciples. It is the feast of the Spirit of all that is holy.

Actually, the word "Easter" was taken from the pagan calendar; the fertility goddess Eostre is honored each year at the Spring Equinox. To celebrate, some Pagans carry out particular rituals. For instance, a woman and a man are chosen to act out the roles of Spring God and Goddess. They play out courtship and symbolically plant seeds. Egg races, egg hunts, egg eating, and egg painting are also traditional activities at this time of year, as the egg is one of Eostre's chief symbols of creation and rebirth.

Summer

Creator, Earth Mother,
we thank you for our lives and
this beautiful day. Thank You for the bright sun
and the rain we received last night.
Thank You for this circle of friends
and the opportunity to be together.
We want to thank You especially at this time
for the giveaway of their lives made by the
chickens, beets, carrots, grains and lettuce.
We thank them for giving of their lives
so we may continue our lives through this
great blessing. Please help us honor them
through how we live our lives.

Native American

Summer festivals are important in the northern parts of earth. Midsummer or Litha means a stopping or standing still of the sun. It is the longest day of the year and the time when the sun is at its maximum elevation. At the summer solstice the light will begin to decrease in the sky and in length. It is also the festival of Li, the Chinese Goddess of light.

As the sun spirals its longest dance,
Cleanse us.

As nature shows bounty and fertility,
Bless us.
Let all things live with loving intent
And to fulfill their truest destiny.

Taken from a Wiccan blessing for Summer

The solstice has had spiritual significance for thousands of years as humans have been amazed by the great power of the sun. The Celts celebrated with bonfires that would add to the sun's energy, while Christians placed the feast of St. John the Baptist towards the end of June.

This is the sun of John the Baptist—he who foretold the Christ. When people came to him asking if he was the Christ he denied it and said that "I must decrease so that He might increase." This is the path of the Christian, to be in denial of self. In the northern lands on this night the people go up into the hills and mountains and build great bonfires to keep the light alive.

Great Spirit, Great Spirit, my Grandfather,
all over the Earth the faces of living things are all alike.
With tenderness have these come up out of the ground.
Look upon these faces of children without number
and with children in their arms
that they may face the winds
and walk the good road to the day of quiet.

"That They May Face the Winds," Black Elk

Times of Our Lives

Prayer ideally should accompany us throughout our life's journey. It should also grow along with us. Many people receive religious instruction when they are children and then never bother to update their faith along with their mind and their emotions. We do not remain with the same arithmetic we learned in the third grade. Why do we think that what we learned of God as youngsters is how we should relate to God as adults? As you journey through the stages of life, ask yourself where your faith life exists today. Is your God the God of a child? Is your prayer still the prayer of a child?

Birth

Certainly the moment of birth leads to prayer for the parents and participants. The miracle of new life brings us back to our roots, to what life is all about and just how precious it is. We reach out to cling to and protect this new member of our family. We give God thanks for the journey we have been through and for the gift of new life.

Religions nearly always have rites to welcome the new infant into the human and spiritual family. We rejoice in the gift of the new child and at the same time officially include them in their new spiritual community.

In the Jewish and Muslim traditions, new males are welcomed into the covenant through the rite of circumcision. In Christianity the new child is baptized or dedicated to God shortly after birth. Through these rituals they are welcomed into the new communities who celebrate their gift to us all.

Father, we thank you for your marvelous gift;
you have allowed us to share in your divine parenthood.
During this time of waiting,
we ask you to protect and nurture
these first mysterious stirrings of life.
May our child come safely
into the light of the world
and to the new birth of baptism.
Mother of God, we entrust our child
to your loving heart. Amen.

"Prayer for an Expectant Mother,"
The Pope's Family Prayer Book

Youth

Lord! Make this youth radiant,
and confer Thy bounty upon this poor creature.
Bestow upon him knowledge,
grant him added strength at the break of every morn
and guard him within the shelter of Thy protection

so that he may be freed from error,
may devote himself to the service of Thy Cause,
may guide the wayward, lead the hapless,
free the captives and awaken the heedless,
that all may be blessed with Thy remembrance and praise.
Thou art the Mighty and the Powerful.
'Abdu'l Bahá

Most spiritual traditions celebrate a person's entry into adulthood. In our own culture, Judaism celebrates a Bar Mitzvah for a young man and, more recently, a Bat Mitzvah for a young woman. These rituals acknowledge that the young person is ready to carry on the duties of an adult in the community. In the Jewish ceremony he or she must read from the Torah—the Scriptures—at the synagogue service.

Hear, O children, the instruction of a parent,
And give attention that you may gain understanding,
For I give you sound teaching;
Do not abandon my instruction.
Acquire wisdom! Acquire understanding!
Do not forget nor turn away from the words of my mouth.
"Do not forsake her, and she will guard you;
Love her, and she will watch over you.
I have directed you in the way of wisdom;
I have led you in upright paths.
When you walk, your steps will not be impeded;

And if you run, you will not stumble.
Take hold of instruction; do not let go.
Guard her, for she is your life.
Graduation blessing, Proverbs 4:1-13

The Christian sacrament of Confirmation has turned into just such a rite of passage. Unfortunately, Confirmation has become a happenstance sacrament. It is really the completion of Baptism—the sacrament of second birth, and to use it as a passage to adulthood forgets its original intention. But that it has become such a powerful passage into adulthood for young Christians shows the need for some acknowledgment of the person's entry into maturity.

Sabbath

In the West one day of the week is set aside for God. For Jews this is the Sabbath—our Saturday. Christians shifted the Sabbath to Sunday to honor the Lord's Resurrection from the dead. For Muslims Friday is the day of prayer when one goes to the mosque for prayers and teaching.

The holy Throne of Glory is united in the secret of One,
prepared for the High Holy King to rest upon Her.
When Sabbath enters She is alone,
separated from the Other Side,
all judgments removed from Her.
Basking in the oneness of holy light,
She is crowned over and over to face the Holy King.

All powers of wrath and masters of judgment flee from Her.

Her face shines with a light from beyond;

She is crowned below by the holy people,

and all of them are crowned with new souls.

Then the beginning of prayer to bless Her with joy and beaming faces:

Barekbu ET YHVH ha-Mevorakh,

"Bless ET YHVH, the-Blessed One,"

ET YHVH, blessing Her first.

Jewish prayer for the entrance of Sabbath

Marriage

All cultures celebrate marriage, and most regard it as a religious event. The couple goes to the place of worship and together with family, friends, and neighbors they enter into a marriage with one another. The different symbols and rituals surrounding marriage are too numerous to detail here.

Certainly marriage is difficult to maintain in our culture. Almost half of marriages end in divorce. One reason is the relaxation in moral standards. But another factor is the length of time people are together today.

A couple of generations ago, the average length of a marriage was five years. Today is it not uncommon for people to remain together over fifty years. And we must make this journey with little or no support from the community.

Our married friends deserve to be remembered in our prayers. Remembering is an important aspect of prayer. As you pray for your family and friends you call them to mind. You bring them into your memory where you can think of them and perhaps be moved to call them or visit.

Prayer can keep us linked to one another. Tell yourself that you will remember those people whose weddings you attend in your prayers. All it takes is a moment and it strengthens your ties to one another.

Blessed art Thou, O Lord our God, King of the Universe,
who created mirth and joy,
bridegroom and bride,
gladness, jubilation, dancing, and delight,
love and brotherhood, peace and fellowship.
Quickly, O Lord our God,
may the sound of mirth and joy
be heard in the streets of Judah and Jerusalem,
the voice of bridegroom and bride,

jubilant voices of bridegrooms from their canopies
and youths from the feasts of song.
Blessed art Thou, O Lord,
who makes the bridegroom rejoice with the bride.
Jewish wedding prayer

Sexual yogas, unfortunately often pursued today out of less than pure interests, are famous. Today they are mostly known from the Hindu and Buddhist worlds where they are part of the tantric traditions.

Tantra was never meant to be for everyone. It is secret, open only to those who have completed rigorous preparation and purification. The tantra uses the powerful sexual energy to break through illusion and allow the disciple to achieve enlightenment in this lifetime.

The sexual yogas are only one form of tantra, although given the prurient interest of some Westerners they have come to be viewed as the entire tantric tradition. They should not be indulged in without the proper training and supervision. There is a tantric saying that whoever practices tantra walks the razor's edge. These are powerful energies that can lead to madness as well as enlightenment.

What the sexual tantras do show us are the power and the sacredness of sexual energy. When Catholic Christianity declares that marriage is a sacrament by which the couple can encounter God, it is pointing to this same power. In intercourse the individual loses his or her sense of separateness and enters into a union with the other experienced as the divine.

Through your love for each other, through learning the art of making one person happy, you learn to express your love for the whole of humanity and all beings.

Thich Nhat Hanh

How is your own experience of sexuality an approach to the divine? Can you call your sexuality holy? Are there obstacles which prevent you from seeing sexuality as a vehicle to bring you to the divine?

Many Westerners are wounded in their sexuality. Sex has often been pronounced evil or dirty in corrupt Western spiritualities. As we seek to regain a healthy holy sexuality it will be only natural that we may swing from one extreme to another—from puritanism to hedonism. As spiritual persons we must attempt to recover our sexuality for our spiritual well being. Sexual touch can be the most intimate moment for us. It can open us not only to the beloved but to God.

Mealtime

Grace at meals is an almost universal custom among religious and spiritual people. To take time to pray before we eat allows us to stand back and acknowledge our food as a gift from God.

Some people stop to acknowledge the immediate giver of the gift—the animal, fruit, or vegetable—which gave its life to bring us life and nourishment. If you are beginning to plan a prayer life give careful consideration to including grace with meals as part of your routine. The following are examples of the wide variety of prayers that you might wish to use, or these may serve as a model for your own grace.

**Blessed art Thou,
Lord our God,
King of the universe
who brings forth
bread from the earth.**

Jewish blessing over bread

This food is the gift of the whole universe,
Each morsel is a sacrifice of life,
May I be worthy to receive it.
May the energy in this food,
Give me the strength,
To transform my unwholesome qualities
into wholesome ones.
I am grateful for this food,
May I realize the Path of Awakening,

For the sake of all beings.

Namu amida butsu

Buddhist mealtime prayer

O Christ God,

bless the food and drink of Thy servants,

for Thou art holy, always, now and ever

and unto ages of ages.

Traditional

O Most Holy Trinity,

have mercy on us!
Lord, cleanse us from our sins!
Master, pardon our transgressions!

Holy One, visit and heal our infirmities
for Thy name's sake.

Glory to the Father, and to the Son, and to the Holy Spirit,
now and ever and unto ages of ages. Amen.

Lord, have mercy! (3 times)

O Christ God, bless the food and drink of Thy servants,
for Thou art holy, always,

now and ever and unto ages of ages.

Traditional Orthodox graces

Bless us O Lord, and these thy gifts,
Which we are about to receive, from thy bounty,
Through Christ, Our Lord.
Amen.

Traditional

God is great and God is Good,
And we thank him for our food;
By His hand we must be fed,
Give us Lord, our daily bread. Amen.

A child's grace

Be present at our table, Lord,
Be here and everywhere adored.
Thy creatures bless, and grant that we
May feast in paradise with thee.

John Wesley

Retreat

A retreat is a time to withdraw from ordinary life so that a person can turn within and through prayer commune with God. It can be structured or not, led or self conducted. Today there are hundreds of opportunities for retreat available throughout the country.

In the spiritual life it is necessary to take time out for retreat. It affords us the opportunity to take a look at our life,

Always keep a place to which you can retreat.

Chinese proverb

reassess our values and goals, and plunge us into the silence of God.

The place of retreat is important. Although you can do a retreat at home or anywhere, it is best to find someplace special—away from the business of daily life, away from your normal associates, certainly away from your normal schedule and for God's sake away from your cell phone.

A retreat center is usually in a beautiful spot of nature so that we might there find the divine. It is a place of quiet—away from the noises of modern life. It is a place for settling down and doing nothing. That can seem like a scary idea to those of us embroiled in the world. And that fear signals just how much we need this time out.

Native American peoples have developed the Vision Quest as a once in a lifetime retreat for a young person. Young boys at puberty enter a period of fasting, meditation, and physical hardship.

Each boy leaves the tribe and goes into a wilderness area on his own. There he hopes to receive a vision that will show him the way he should live. He hopefully also finds a spirit who will accompany him throughout his life.

The shaman also undergoes a perilous voyage to encounter the spirits. He must turn inward and confront his inner demons. He returns from his initiation healed and bearing gifts for his people to help them in their life and healing.

Parenting

O Lord, omnipotent Father,
we give you thanks for having given us children.
They are our joy,
and we accept with serenity the worries, fears,
and labors which bring us pain.
Help us to love them sincerely.
Through us you gave life to them;
from eternity you knew them and loved them.
Give us the wisdom to guide them,
patience to teach them,
vigilance to accustom them to the good
through our example.

"Parents' Prayer for Their Children," St. Charles Borromeo Catholic Church, Picayune, Mississippi

Parenting brings many to prayer as they exhaust their own wisdom and resources. In parenting we see the extent of love—the measure of love we have for our children. We give thanks for that love—beyond all telling. We ask for guidance. What do we do? What do we say? Are we keeping the channels of communication open?

Parenting is a two-person job even though for many today it is a solitary vocation. Take some time to pray with your spouse over the family. This prayer doesn't need a lot of words. Just hold each child in your imagination. Pray for their happiness and safekeeping. Perhaps there are things you want to say about this child. Any fears? Any desires? How can you

God, make me **brave for life,** oh, braver than this. **Let me straighten** after pain, as a tree straightens after the rain, **Shining** and **lovely again.**

Grace Noll Crowell

support each other in raising your children? You do not need answers to the prayer. The prayer itself is a process whereby you can dedicate the family and yourselves to God.

Lord Jesus Christ,
Good Shepherd of the sheep,
you gather the lambs in your arms
and carry them in your bosom:
We commend to your loving care this child ____________.
Relieve his pain, guard him from all danger,
restore to him your gifts of gladness and strength,
and raise him up to a life of service to you.
Hear us, we pray, for your dear Name's sake. Amen.

"For a Sick Child," Book of Common Prayer

Then there is the question of how you are going to raise your children in prayer. Do you pray with them? Do you teach prayers appropriate for their ages? Do you answer their questions about God and the spiritual life? Do you attend services with them? Are they enrolled in religious education? What are your hopes for your children's spiritual growth and development?

Sickness and Health

Sickness is probably the most powerful pull to prayer: both our own sickness and that of our loved ones. As the old saying goes, "There are no atheists in the trenches." When we are very sick we reach the end of our ropes. Our resources are exhausted. Fear eats away at us. We are helpless. Illness is not something most of us handle well.

Studies find prayer can be a powerful tool in sickness. First of all, to be open to healing from God includes being open to healing from the medical staff. Our attitude toward our healing is an important part of the process. Why do some people survive while others succumb to the same disease? Could not a large part of the answer be attitude?

The sickness of friends and family also calls us to faith. We want to pray for their healing. Perhaps we come to prayer as a last resort. Or maybe we believe strongly in prayer's power to heal.

The healing and the spiritual arts are joined together in Eastern traditions. The doctor is one of both body and spirit. As we follow the urge to pray for our friends we are joining with our brothers and sisters everywhere. We come to the only One who truly has power over life and death. We come with our hopes and

May I become a medicine for the sick and their physician, their support until sickness come not again.

Santideva

wishes. We come out of our hurt and our pain. Who could be on your own prayer list?

Watch, O Lord, with those who wake,
or watch, or weep tonight,
and give your angels charge over those who sleep.
Tend your sick ones, O Lord Christ.
Rest your weary ones.
Bless your dying ones.
Soothe your suffering ones.
Pity your afflicted ones.
Shield your joyous ones.
And for all your love's sake.
Amen.

St. Augustine

EXERCISE

You might want to include a healing meditation as part of your prayer. Here you can pray for those close to you and for anyone who might have asked for your prayers. This exercise takes between ten and twenty minutes and should be done in a nice quiet place.

Begin by sitting up. Close your eyes. Take a couple of deep breaths and let go. Now begin at the toes. Just sense them. If you cannot sense them then imagine you can. That is enough. Now continue to move up and sense each part of your body until you reach the top of your head.

Now imagine God standing before you. What is the most powerful healing image of God for you? Picture that person or symbol. Imagine God there. Be playful. Don't try too hard. Imagine God sitting opposite you. Imagine healing energy flowing from God's heart or God's center to your own heart and from there throughout your body—top to toe.

When you are ready, imagine the sick person or persons for whom you are praying between you and God. They can be sitting down or any way you want to picture them. Now imagine that healing light is pouring out of God and through your sick friend and into your own heart. Stay with the light. Allow it to flow back and forth between you and God.

When you space out, come back to the practice. Don't blame yourself. That's counterproductive. You are doing fine. Wandering happens. In fact if you do not space out you are probably trying too hard. Relax. Let God in.

When you are ready to conclude the practice first allow the image of the sick person or persons to disappear. Now the energy is flowing from God to your heart and body. Now allow the energy to cease. Imagine all the energy now in your body flowing down and out through your feet into the ground. When you are ready, conclude with a prayer to God. You could give thanks for being included in this ministry. Pray for your friend. Pray for those in healing professions.

A sick man was once asked
why he did not ask God to heal him
of his affliction.
He replied,
"First, I am sure that our loving God
would not have made me sick
if it were not best for me.
Second, it would be wrong
to wish for my will rather than
God's will for me.
Third, why should
I ask the rich, loving and generous God
for such a small thing?"

Meister Eckhardt

Death

O Allah, forgive and have mercy on him
(or her).

Grant him ease and respite.

Make his resting place a noble
one, and facilitate his entry.

Cleanse him with water, snow
and coolness,

and purify him of wrong
doings, as a white cloth is
purified of grime.

Grant him an abode finer than
his worldly one,

and grant him entrance to Paradise

and protect him from the chastisement of
the grave,

and protect him from the chastisement of the Fire.

Muslim funeral prayer

Death brings us all to prayer because it brings us to the edge of our being. It shocks and threatens us. It reveals our own vulnerability. It shakes our life and our well being. And it is so absolutely final.

Yet it does not stifle us. We find ourselves praying through our pain and fear. We pray first of course for our loved one. Keep them safe. Let them know how much we love them. We then pray for all the departed. We shall share their fate someday.

Naked you came from Earth the Mother. Naked you return to her. May a good wind be your road.

"The Return to Mother Earth," Omaha tribe

Finally we pray for ourselves and the community of mourners. Be with us in this hour of trial. Help us to comfort one another. Help us to keep the memory fresh and support one another in this time of suffering.

Death,
O my mother Nut,
Stretch your wings over me,
Let me become like the imperishable stars,
Like the indefatigable stars—
May Nut extend her arms over me
And her name of
"She who extends her arms,
Chases away the shadows,
And makes the Light shine everywhere."

Egyptian, from an inscription on a coffin lid in the Louvre

EXERCISE

We have looked at the various times of prayer. To conclude, take some time to consider what will be your own times for prayer.

What times of day most draw you to prayer? How can you begin to make them the beginning of a prayer practice? Do not overdo it. Start small. After all you probably have to create this new life on your own, at least at the present.

What times and seasons are important for your spiritual life? What times do you celebrate? Are there seasons when it is good for you to be active and others when it is beneficial to withdraw into solitude?

What do you wish to bring into the present from your own past? Are there certain prayers or prayer practices that have been important on your spiritual journey? How can you honor them now in your practice?

Take some time to consider what prayer life you want. We will return to this project as we go through the book. Today we are only looking at the times of prayer. What routine is possible and valuable for you today? You can of course change this contract any time as you embark on the journey.

chapter**four**

exploring a great spiritual practice

The Places of Prayer

Now we are going to explore prayer by exploring the different things and behavior surrounding prayer. After all, we have said just about all there is to be said about prayer itself. Embrace the Real. Pray. Pray. Pray.

But there is more to prayer than the simple prayer itself. We have already considered the Object of Prayer. And you have begun to reach out to the Real in your own words and through the benefit of the other prayers we have prayed as we entered another's spiritual path.

Let us now consider where our prayer takes place. Of course it can take place any place a human can go. And the places of prayer are varied and many.

Home

When all is said and done the primary place of prayer will probably be your home. And there it may be either solitary or familial. It may also be a place of feast or a fast. What ways of praying together might you practice in your house?

Consider the physical house. Where is there a place of prayer in that building? Is there a place of rest and quiet? It doesn't have to be there already. It can be blessed into being. Where do you feel the presence of God? Where do you feel most comfortable? We will return later to how you are going to establish your prayer place when we consider the aids to prayer. For now, can you pray here?

Peace be to this house And to all who dwell in it. Peace be to them that enter And to them that depart.

Blessing for the home

Nature

Nature in her many facets has always called us to the holy and to prayer. Where do you find the holy in your environment?

Find a nature space: a place where nature is still untroubled. Surely you can at least find a park, hopefully with a garden. I myself would try to be at a seashore. But there are mountains on the other hand, and plains with great lakes upon them.

Find your sacred spot, and spend some time there. Why is it sacred for you? Is it a piece of land your family owned? A cottage? Wherever this sacred space is for you, spend time here. Be silent here. Listen to God here.

What importance does the sun have to your sacred spot? Can you see the sun from here? Are you hidden in shadow? The position of the sun is a key factor in establishing any sacred spot.

Look at Stonehenge. So much labor for a calendar. Western churches were built with their faces towards the East and the rising sun. The tall, thin windows behind the altar and facing East were filled with golden glass. These Christians were building a holy geography.

Then there is the moon. Since the moon waxes and wanes and has such power over both seas and spirits, she has been worshiped and called sacred.

Begin to make friends with the moon. Do you know what phase the moon is in right now? Are we approaching full moon or departing from it? Go find the moon. What can she tell you about the sacred?

City

And did those feet in ancient time
Walk upon England's mountains green?
And was the holy Lamb of God
On England's pleasant pastures seen?
And did the Countenance Divine
Shine forth upon our clouded hills?
And was Jerusalem builded here
Among these dark Satanic mills?
Bring me my bow of burning gold:
Bring me my arrows of desire:
Bring me my spear: O clouds unfold!
Bring me my chariot of fire.
I will not cease from mental fight,
Nor shall my sword sleep in my hand
Till we have built Jerusalem
In England's green and pleasant land.

"Jerusalem," William Blake

The first cities were holy cities. And in their very center they erected the temple—the dwelling place of God. Today there are still holy cities to which believers dream of making pilgrimage. For Muslims this city is Mecca; one of the five pillars of Islam requires each Muslim, if possible, to make the pilgrimage to Mecca.

Jerusalem is the holy city to all three Western faiths Jews, Christians, and Muslims. For Catholic Christians Rome has become another holy city and the center for their church. Hindus consider Benares to be a holy city. And Tibetan Buddhists placed Lhasa at the center of their faith.

In addition to the holy city, there is the shrine: a holy spot. It could be some saint's birthplace, such as Assisi for St. Francis. It could commemorate some event, such as the rock where Mohammed received the Koran. Like the holy cities, people flock to shrines to draw near the holy. The architecture of the shrine is often sculpted to help the pilgrim enter into prayer.

Temple

We may have to resort to our imaginations to explore the temple, especially the temple of animal sacrifice. If there is a temple available in your neighborhood, visit it. And visit a synagogue, a church, and a mosque. No hurry. But these are places of prayer. If you want help praying, these are the places to go.

The temple appears throughout human culture. It is the home of God, the dwelling place of God on earth. There are really no such temples today. The temple has been civilized and is not its original self. The most famous temple in Jerusalem was destroyed two thousand years ago. This was the dwelling place of YHWH and pilgrims came from all over to celebrate the great feasts such as Passover.

In the old days the temple would be a place of sacrifice. In the Jerusalem temple animals were sold in huge numbers. The sewers were literally rivers of blood. The sacrifice brought the worshipper into right relation with God by fulfilling the ritual demands.

The temple has been revived by the Mormons. The primary Mormon temple is in Salt Lake City, but there are other temples scattered throughout the Mormon world. These temples are closed to non-Mormons, although they are open for visitation before they are consecrated. Mormons go to the temple to celebrate marriage in eternity and for the baptism of the dead, which is a major mission in their faith. Like other temples these are the holiest places of their faith.

There was never an image of God in the Jerusalem temple since God could not be imagined and the religion forbade idolatry. But other temples will have as their central focus the image of the God or Buddha.

If you have the chance to visit a temple, do so as an experience of prayer. How does this space open you up to the divine? How do you experience the divine here? What does this temple tell you about the divine?

Synagogue

In the West the synagogue and the church are daughters to the temple. The synagogue began as the local gathering place for a Jewish congregation. There they could say prayers, study the Torah—the sacred Law—and also meet for social occasions.

This was never the function of the temple that was in Jerusalem. But after the temple was destroyed for the second time, the synagogue became the primary focus for community worship. The house is the primal place of Jewish worship today. The synagogue compliments the home as a prayer space.

Take some time to visit a synagogue. Do so for a Sabbath service. Ask a Jewish friend to take you so he or she can answer any questions. You will notice that the primary focus is up front. This is where the Torah is displayed during services. The Torah is the voice of God to His people, so it is to be honored with pride of place.

Church

The Christian church is the other building to succeed the temple. In the Orthodox and Catholic traditions the church is the successor to the temple, for God indeed does dwell within each church. He does this under the form of consecrated communion bread, which believers believe to be God present. As you enter a church you should easily spot the tabernacle containing the consecrated bread. It will be set off with candles and probably occupy a side altar if it is not in the center itself.

Let the words of my mouth, and the meditation of my heart be acceptable in thy sight, O Lord, my rock and my redeemer.

Psalm 19:14

An Orthodox church will be much more developed than the typical Western church. There will be a screen across the front of the church. The Sacred Mysteries are performed behind this screen. There are no chairs. People stand or kneel for service. And services can be long.

The church is decorated in holy pictures called icons. These are not meant to be true to life. Rather they project the holy in the saint or divinity. Take some time to visit an

Orthodox church in your area. How does the church speak to you of God?

The Catholic church is different from the Orthodox in a number of ways. First the saints are found in holy pictures and in statues as well. The center of the church is the altar. As you enter the church, you will find the baptismal font where a person becomes a Christian through the sacrament of Baptism. You will find chairs in Europe, and in America pews which were adopted from Protestant churches.

We need to clarify among the various Christian churches. In general we can distinguish three major traditions—the Orthodox, the Catholic, and the Protestant. The confusion arises with the catholic tradition. This includes but is not necessarily limited to the Roman Catholic church. Some churches in the Protestant tradition are also catholic, notably the Episcopal and Anglican churches. Other Protestant churches are catholic in confession, provided they cling to the Nicene Creed—these would include the Lutheran and Methodist churches. When we refer specifically to the Roman Catholic church we will use the full title. But catholic refers to all of these catholic communions.

Again, take some time to visit a Catholic church. Attend services on a Sunday along with a Catholic friend so they can answer your questions. All of these faiths are very happy to welcome visitors. They would like you to understand how they worship God.

A modern Protestant church shouldn't be too great a change from the Catholic church. Both bodies of churches are overcoming their differences and finding their way to a common worship. There is probably an altar, even if it is only a table. The pulpit may be more prominent. The Protestant focus is on God's Word. The organ may be quite prominent as well as the choir. The Protestant approaches God in song, and those hymns have expressed for hundreds of years what Christians say to God.

Mosque

Most communities in America today have a mosque. Chances are you have been in a church and even a synagogue. But have you been to a mosque? Go. You do not have to go for the formal prayers. But that would enable you to experience how this place draws the Muslim to God.

The mosque is not a temple. For the Muslim, it is all important that prayer should flow toward Mecca. So the mosque is oriented toward the sacred city. Like the temple you remove your shoes. You are entering the holy. The space is probably very plain. There is no altar, not even a place for the Qur'an. God is praised in the word here. And the word is Arabic, the Holy Language.

How does this place speak to you of God? There are no images here. Nothing can mediate God to humanity. There may, however, be nonrepresentational art and beautiful arabesques. What does this place speak to you concerning God?

Sweat Lodge

The sweat lodge is a place of prayer and healing for many Native American peoples. It is found in other cultures as well. A typical lodge is made of young saplings bent into a half dome and covered with blankets, skins, or canvas. There is a round pit in the center tended by a leader and fire keeper. The leader is the teacher; the fire keeper has many different functions. The ceremony will combine the elements of fire, wood, water, and stone.

To begin, the participants enter in a clockwise direction. Traditionally men and women keep separate sweats. The rocks, which have been heated outside, are brought into the lodge by the fire keeper and placed in the central pit by the leader. The sweat lodge door is then closed and the interior heats up.

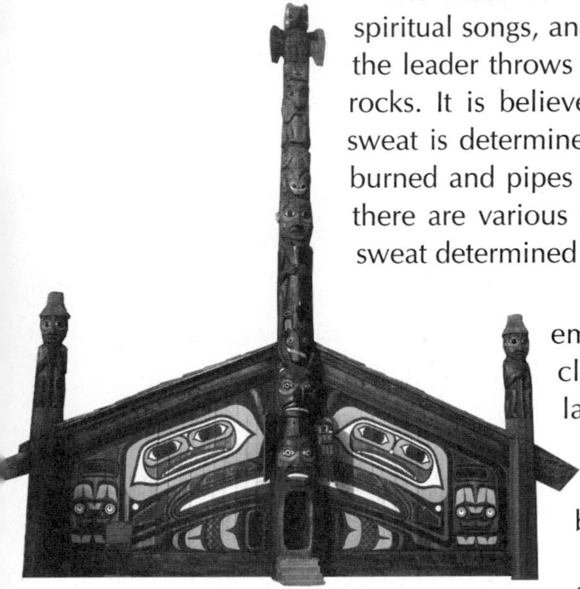

The ritual consists of four rounds of prayers, spiritual songs, and drumming. From time to time the leader throws water and herbs on the heated rocks. It is believed that the temperature of the sweat is determined by the spirits. Sweet grass is burned and pipes are smoked as offerings. Today there are various possible rituals performed in a sweat determined by the leader.

At the conclusion, the people emerge from the lodge in a clockwise direction. They then lay down on the grass to cool off. It is said that you emerge from the sweat lodge like a newborn baby. The sweat lodge symbolizes a woman's womb. Or the sweat lodge may represent the universe and connect the people to the past, the earth, and the spirit world. In addition to the more spiritual uses, sweats are also an opportunity for friends and kinsmen to spend time together in a quiet, contemplative setting.

Rather than going to church, I attend a sweat lodge;
rather than accepting bread and toast
[sic] from the Holy Priest,
I smoke a ceremonial pipe to come into
Communion with the Great Spirit;
and rather than kneeling

with my hands placed together in prayer,
I let sweet grass be feathered over my entire being
for spiritual cleansing
and allow the smoke to carry
my prayers into the heavens.
I am a Mi'kmaq, and this is how we pray.

Noah Augustine, "Grandfather was a knowing Christian," *Toronto Star*

Again, take some time to consider where you will pray. Of course you do not have to choose just one place. But begin with your daily prayer.

Is there a place you can go within your house or nearby where you can draw close to God? It does not have to be big—a corner of a room could serve.

And when you go to a public place of prayer, where do you want to go? What building or shrine speaks to you of the holy? For now, decide upon a place.

EXERCISE

Here is an exercise to help you find your sacred space. You may do it in a sacred building or you might do it in your own home. The exercise should take about twenty minutes. Do it in a time when you can be alone and uninterrupted.

First take a seat and close your eyes. Take a few deep breaths and relax. As you exhale, imagine you are breathing out all the tension and the things on your mind.

Go to a place that you may want to make a prayer place. Take a few minutes to relax and center here and now. Continue to take slow deep breaths. Allow them to touch each part of your body and bring relaxation. Then, when you are ready, begin this exercise.

Open your eyes. Observe your environment. Where do you feel the holy? Move around. Try out different spots. Can you feel the difference? Be open to the process. Where does the sacred manifest for you? When you are done, consider how you might make this space your own sacred place of prayer.

exploring a great spiritual practice

chapterfive

The Tools of Prayer

Throughout the ages people have used tangible things and methods to aid their prayers. Such aids include special clothing, food, altars and prayer rugs, incense, pictures, music, and dance. Others have found that these objects actually distract from prayer. They keep us busy but do not lead us to the heart of prayer—the opening of ourselves to the divine. These people prefer to keep their prayer simple and free from any aids.

What does your faith tradition say about prayer aids? As we examine these prayer tools, ask yourself what you feel will help you pray. This is not a question answered once for all. As you progress along your prayer journey, from time to time you will want to reexamine your prayer life. Are the aids you use leading you deeper into prayer? Or have they become a distraction? Do they substitute a false prayer for true prayer? Has prayer become mechanical or rote?

Vestments

One of the first things we might examine is the custom throughout the East to remove the shoes before entering a place of prayer or before prayer itself. It is a sign of humility. "Humble" comes from the Latin word "humus" referring to the earth. When I am humble, I am far from humiliated. I am simply walking upon the earth. I am in touch with who I am and what I am about. The Catholic poet Gerard Manley Hopkins used the image of shoes as a metaphor for our alienation: "Nor can foot feel being shod."

Throughout history people have removed their shoes in the presence of the holy. Abraham, the ancestor of Jews, Christians, and Muslims, was asked to remove his shoes when he came upon God in the burning bush.

Next time you pray, take off your shoes. What does it do for your prayer? Could the casting off of shoes bring you more in touch with yourself and God? What does this say about where you are? We are so used to our shoes. We have them on from the time we get up until we go to bed. What happens when we remove them in the presence of the Lord?

Orthodox Jewish men use a prayer shawl and phylacteries to help them enter into a proper atmosphere of prayer. Phylacteries are small boxes filled with prayers which the man ties to his forehead and his left arm. He then pulls the prayer shawl over his head. The shawl separates him from the world so that he might enter into the interior world of prayer.

In your own search for a prayer life, what helps you to move from the outer to the inner world? It can be a shawl, shoes, a special place, or a short prayer itself. Of course none of these methods are necessary. And we need to stay aware of a tendency to allow the props to replace the prayer. But what helps you to enter into the sacred world?

The Muslim uses a prayer rug to perform his or her prayer. He will also remove his shoes. The rug, of course, serves a very practical purpose of protecting the worshipper from dirt. But it also can serve as a reminder that he or she is moving from the secular world into the sacred.

Some people such as the Amish or Muslims use dress as a way to separate themselves from the rest of the world. Here the dress becomes not just a vestment for prayer but a sign to the person and the world that this person is set aside for God. Dress used in this way was more pronounced in the past among Catholic religious people. These brothers and sisters had dedicated their lives to following God, and their clothing signaled this to the world. Today you may find such religious habits, as they are called, only among those religious who withdraw from the world to monasteries and convents—houses of prayer for men or women. It also survives in the Roman collar, which is the sign of a priest.

Such apparel goes far beyond a vestment for prayer and becomes a sign to the world of the person's state of life. It is also found throughout the East among monks and nuns. Here, too, color becomes important. In the West color is pretty much limited to black. But in Buddhism the color can be either yellow or maroon depending upon the culture. Yellow is found throughout Southeast Asia and maroon identifies a Tibetan monk.

Dress becomes key in the celebration of public worship. Few faith communities do not employ some form of vestment. In some Protestant churches it may be a simple robe. In Catholic and Orthodox churches, vestments can become quite elaborate. Again, donning a vestment is a way of passing over from the secular to the sacred. In past Catholic tradition the minister prayed certain prayers as he vested to turn his mind from the everyday to the holy.

Finally, you might want to explore the experience of praying naked. This occurs among some yogis. The state of nakedness emphasizes our vulnerability. We stand naked before God. We no longer choose to hide who we are from God.

It can also be a way of reclaiming our bodies. We Westerners, largely due to defective spiritualities, are alienated from our bodies. We are ashamed of them like Adam and Eve, our first father and mother, after they had sinned. Indeed we came to see the effects of sin in our bodies and especially in our sex.

But our bodies are God's creations. They are good and beautiful. And they are beautiful in a way far beyond our obsession with youth and Hollywood physiques.

What is your own relation to your body? Are you ashamed of your body? Do you regard your body as dirty or sinful? Can you give thanks to God for the gift of your body?

Beyond the mere facticity of our body, humanity has found ways to pray with the body. This is something we will explore further on in our journey. For now explore how you might best pray naked. It is going to be different from the way you pray clothed. Have a sense of play. What is the best way for you to pray naked? Lying down? Standing up? Sitting? Kneeling? What is the experience of feeling the air upon your skin like? What about the lightness—no clothing to hold you down?

Food and Fasting

Since food is such a focal part of our lives it is only natural that it be taken up into our religious and spiritual lives. There are two ways in which food is connected with prayer. First of all, as we saw above there is the custom of giving thanks or saying grace over our meals. But food often takes an even more essential place in the spiritual life. And

then by abstaining from food we can also seek to draw closer to God.

Catholic Christians center their faith around the last meal Jesus shared with his disciples. Bread and wine are blessed and then consumed by the faithful in obedience to Jesus' command to remember him.

Almost all Christian churches observe this ritual. They differ in the place they give it and in how they understand it. That meal was probably itself part of the Jewish Passover, which remembers Israel's liberation from slavery in Egypt.

Sacrifice is central to almost all religions. Traditionally it involved the sacrifice of some plant or animal to the God and then a communion of the leftovers among the worshippers. The sacrifice demonstrates our thanks for God's many blessings. The meal allows us to share in the bounty of God.

May the Lord accept this, our offering, and bless our food that it may bring us strength in our body, vigor in our mind, and selfless devotion in our hearts for His service.

Swami Paramananda

Jews observe the beginning of Sabbath—on Saturdays—with a holy meal. The family gathers together to usher in the Sabbath when they will refrain from work and enjoy their companionship and the companionship of God.

Some traditions keep festivals to their God, which often involve food and drink. And certain feasts often call for special foods and drink. Our own Thanksgiving calls for a turkey, stuffing, and cranberries to be a "real" Thanksgiving. Orthodox Christians celebrate Easter with special breads and cakes. Christians prepare for Lent with hot cross buns, or, in the Polish tradition, special doughnuts called paczki.

While food may be part of our prayer life, fasting equally finds a place. In a fast, just as in retreat or pilgrimage, we withdraw from our normal routine.

Fasting brings a sacrificial dimension to prayer. Biblical fasting is most often the abstaining from food for a spiritual purpose; and there are various ways to fast. Some people also "fast" a nonfood item.

The fast first of all purifies the body. After a couple days on a real fast you feel different—clearer, cleaner. The poisons accumulated in normal life are eliminated.

We learn to depend not on food for sustenance but on God. We experience the hungers of our poor brothers and sisters and find solidarity with them. And if we fast long enough the change in our metabolism causes a change in consciousness, and we experience communion with God.

Fasting is a noble spiritual practice and should form a part of any serious spiritual life. We may choose to fast at certain holy times. Christians fast during Lent; Jews fast as part of Yom Kippur; Muslims fast during Ramadan. Fasting with other believers helps us find solidarity.

If you do fast you must decide what kind of fast you will keep. A total fast would restrict one to water alone. One should not limit one's intake of water for health reasons. It is all right to engage in a fast from food for three days provided one is in good health. A longer fast should only be undertaken with a doctor's approval and supervision. Most traditions suggest a modified fast where some food or a certain kind of food is allowed.

Here are some fasting options:

A partial food fast refers to giving up either a meal or two or a type of food (like meat) over a period of time.

- give up one meal a day, each day of the entire prayer week
- give up two meals on two days (Wednesday and Friday) of the prayer week

This ritual is one.
The food is one.
We who offer the food are one.
The fire of hunger is also one.
All action is one.
We who understand this are one.

Traditional Hindu blessing over food

- give up two meals a day (breakfast and lunch) each day of the entire prayer week
- give up meat or some other specific food category for the entire week

A full food fast refers to giving up all food except water and/or juices over a period of time.

- give up food, drinking only water and juices for 24 hours
- give up all solid foods for the entire prayer week, drinking only water and juices (Do this under a physician's care.)

An absolute food fast is refraining from both food and drink, but should only be done for three days.

Nonfood fasts include giving up something (such as television) that interferes with your spiritual life.

- give up television or entertainment media for the week

- give up something that distracts you from prayer and spiritual pursuits

Jews fast on Yom Kippur—the only fast day decreed in the Bible. It is a complete, twenty-five-hour fast beginning before sunset on the evening before Yom Kippur and ending after nightfall on the day of Yom Kippur. Jews refrain from eating and drinking (even water) on Yom Kippur. It is a day set aside to "afflict the soul," to atone for the sins of the past year.

On Yom Kippur Jews focus on spiritual elevation. One way to do this is to abstain from the physical such as food, sex, work, material possessions, and superficial pleasures. More specifically, these five physical activities are forbidden on Yom Kippur:

- eating and drinking
- marital relations
- washing
- wearing leather shoes
- applying lotions

Most Christians today observe the season of Lent. This is done above all by fasting. The Roman Catholic rules state that one must restrict food to one main meal a day, accompanied by two smaller meals. There is no food taken between meals.

Since the 1991 World Methodist Conference in Singapore, Methodists around the world have been encouraged by World Methodist Evangelism to participate in the same weekly fast that John Wesley observed most of his life.

In this **water**, I invoke the presence of **holy waters** from the rivers Ganga, Yamuna, Godavari, Saraswati, Narmada, Sindhu, and Kaveri.

Hindu prayer while bathing

Each Thursday evening, after the evening meal, until mid-afternoon on each Friday, Methodist people are invited to follow Wesley's example of fasting and prayer. During this time he did not take solid food but fasted and focused much of his time in prayer.

Muslims fast during the holy month of Ramadan by refraining from food during the daylight. They eat small meals before sunrise and after sunset. They refrain from food during the day. Here is their traditional fasting prayer:

O Allah, on this day,
make my fasts the fasts of those who fast (sincerely),
and my standing up in prayer of those
who stand up in prayer (obediently),
awaken me in it from the sleep of the heedless,
and forgive me my sins, O God of the worlds.
and forgive me, O one who forgives the sinners.

Recited on the first day of Ramadan

Water

Water is an almost universal aid to prayer for its obvious meaning of cleansing and purification. Muslims cleanse their hands and feet before the five times of daily prayer. Jews traditionally entered a ritual bath—the Mikveh—before entering the temple. Catholic Christians bless themselves with holy water upon entering a church. This water is not just for purification but to recall the rite of Baptism—the bath by which a person becomes a Christian.

You may consider a small bowl of water at your place of prayer. It can help you pass over from the secular into the world of prayer as it does for the Christian entering a church. And at the same time it prepares you for prayer through purification.

Altar

Offer only lovely things on my altars—
the bread of life, and jewels,
and feathers, and flowers.
Let the streams of life flow in peace.
Turn from violence.
Learn to think for a long time how to change this world,
how to make it better to live in.
All the people in the world ought to talk about it
and speak well of it always.

Then it will last forever,
and the flowers will bloom forever,
and I will come to you again.

Quetzalcoatl

Altars appear wherever humanity has stopped to pray. We see altars throughout the Hebrew scriptures culminating in the temple Israel erects to God in Jerusalem. The altar is the place where heaven and earth meet—the place where humanity meets God. It is the navel—the center of the world.

The altar is the place of sacrifice. Here we bring our offerings to God. The sacrifice was often bloody in ancient days—a ram, a heifer. Agricultural societies would bring the grain for whose harvest the people prayed.

For the Jew the altar finally became the one altar in the Jerusalem temple. Until that is restored Israel cannot offer sacrifice.

For the Christian the primal altar is the cross upon which Jesus was crucified as he became the sacrifice to end all sacrifices. Many Christians believe this altar should not be duplicated. For other more catholic churches an altar in the church represents that ur-altar. And it is designated with a cross to refer to the primal place of sacrifice. For these Christians the sacrifice that takes place in the Eucharist is not a duplication of the original sacrifice on the cross but a mystical participation in that original sacrifice.

The altar is not found in Islam. But the idea of sacrifice is, however, echoed in the idea of submission to God. The idea of the altar being the center is found in praying toward the holy city of Mecca.

Altars are found throughout the Hindu world. Although they may still be places of sacrifice, there is usually present as well the spiritual sacrifice. As humanity has evolved spiritually we have moved from the idea of the external sacrifice of an animal, grain, or fruit to the spiritual meaning of sacrifice—an offering of the human heart to God—submitting to God as the Muslim does.

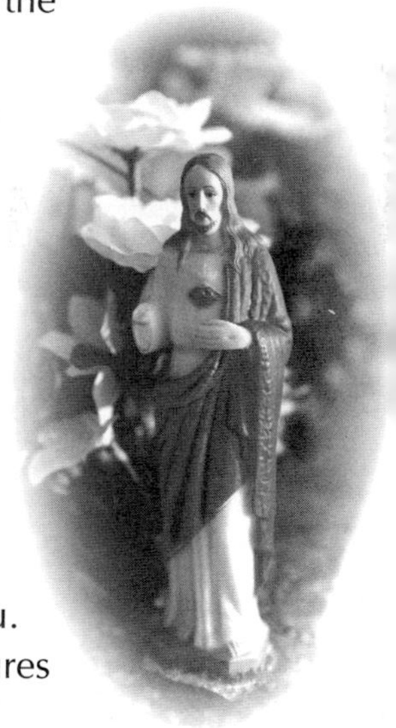

As you contemplate building a place of prayer, do you want an altar? It can focus your spiritual energies. It can serve as a reminder of what the holy means to you. People often decorate their altars with images and pictures of their spiritual mentors and saints. Again, as with every aid to prayer the altar should never distract from what it is there to promote—communion with God. If it takes away from that communication it becomes an idol—putting itself in the place of the divinity.

Seats for Prayer

While you can simply sit or kneel on the earth for prayer, a number of seats have been developed to aid in prayer. Eastern Christian monks use a small stool upon which they sit to practice the Jesus Prayer. This stool was close to the ground to symbolize the worshiper's humility. In Christian churches today you find benches called pews. These were originally found in courtrooms and symbolize the worshipers' being before the Judge.

In the East Buddhists and Hindus have developed cushions to help a person maintain a sitting posture. The Japanese use what are called zafus. Tibetans use a larger cushion that can be folded in a number of ways to support the kneeling or sitting posture chosen. Then there is also the Japanese wooden bench: you place your buttocks on the bench and bend your feet under you. The bench allows the blood to continue to flow to your legs, and the gentle incline of the seat helps maintain an upright posture.

The prayer rug assumes some of the meaning of the altar in prayer. It separates a sacred space from the world. It has an advantage over an altar in being portable. It is most prominent in the Muslim community but appears elsewhere too. It also serves a more practical purpose of keeping the worshiper clean.

Om Ah Hum Vajra Guru Padma Siddhi Hum

Tibetan Buddhist Guru mantra

It also appears in Hinduism as the mat upon which you practice yoga. Here again it keeps you clean. But it is also an outer means of symbolizing the passing over from the secular into the sacred.

Prayer Beads

While the Catholic rosary and Muslim prayer beads are the most widely known prayer beads, these too are found throughout the world of prayer.

The Christian rosary has an interesting history. The Christians' chief book of prayer is the Book of Psalms—the collection of 150 of Israel's prayers. Still today these prayers form the kernel of daily prayer for the Catholic Christian.

However, in the Dark Ages when literacy was rare the idea arose that the worshipper could substitute a short prayer for the Psalms, and praying that prayer would be equivalent to praying the Psalms. The fifty beads of the rosary could help him or her count the prayers. Three times around the circle and the person would have prayed 150 prayers—the equivalent of a psaltery.

Hail Mary full of grace,
The Lord is with you.
Blessed are you among women
and blessed is the fruit of your womb, Jesus.

Holy Mary,
mother of God,
pray for us sinners, now
and at the hour of our death. Amen.

Ave Maria

While the final prayer is more complicated than that—adding meditations upon the life of Jesus and Mary—the rosary itself is simply a device for counting prayers. And it shares this with all other prayer beads. But, more than a counter, it helps center the person in prayer. It is easy to drift off from prayer. The beads in one's hands help one stay focused. Of course it is possible to still drift away—nothing is perfect.

How to Pray the Rosary

Traditional Rosary
See Web: www.familyrosary.org/main/rosary-how.php
For an Ecumenical Rosary appropriate to all Christians
See Web:
www.ecumenicalrosary.org

Prayer Flags and Prayer Wheels

Prayer flags and wheels are familiar today thanks to Tibetan Buddhism, where they play a key role. Prayer flags have mantras printed upon them. And prayer wheels contain mantras inside. Tibetan Buddhists believe the mantras have spiritual power. They believe that the power manifests while the mantras are properly prayed, as well as when the wind hits the flag and water or wind turns the wheel.

I was once present as a lama explained how these prayer implements work. The wheels and flags generate spiritual power which protects the people. When he was challenged about whether they actually worked, he replied,

Om mani padme hum.

Tibetan Buddhist mantra

"Sometimes it works, sometimes it doesn't." Whether prayer flags and other prayer aids are authentic or relics of superstition is something you will have to explore and answer for yourself.

Candles and Incense

Blessed are you, Lord, our God,
king of the universe who has sanctified us
with His commandments
and commanded us
to light the candles of Shabbat.
Jewish prayer

Candles also serve as aids to prayer. Originally candles had a much more practical purpose of lighting the space. Did meditation upon this practical source of illumination lead to its spiritual significance? Or was that spiritual meaning present all along? Look at the words themselves—light, illumination, enlightenment. How intimately joined they are to our spiritual project!

But in addition to its practical purpose of supplying light, the candle itself becomes a focus of prayer. Meditation upon the candle is found throughout the spiritual worlds. Gazing upon the light allows us to empty our minds and draws us into the presence of God. Like water, light is a universal symbol for the divine. The Tibetan Book of the Dead describes the end of our spiritual journey as going into the Great White Light. Christians call Jesus the Light of the World. So it is only natural that candles would be used to draw us toward God.

Incense is also an almost universal prayer object. The Psalm says, "May my evening prayer rise like incense before you O Lord." The sweetness of the incense reminds us of the savor of God. The smoke rising up to the sky, as the psalmist noted, echoes our prayer also rising up to God. And the stick of incense, like the candle, is an image of sacrifice—both are spent in the service of prayer. Finally, just as the candle originally served a more practical purpose, the incense originally covered over the earthy odors of our early ancestors. It is wonderful to see how so many of these prayer tools evolved from a very practical use to embrace a spiritual meaning.

Bells and Chimes

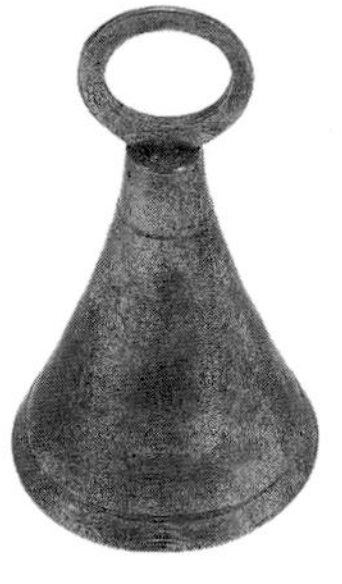

Bells form a part of our prayer lives throughout almost all human cultures. Church bells have traditionally called Christians to prayer. And in the catholic traditions a special prayer, the Angelus, has called the faithful to prayer at dawn (6 a.m.), noon, and dusk (6 p.m.).

Verse: The Angel of the Lord declared unto Mary.
Response: And she conceived of the Holy Spirit.
Hail Mary, etc.

V. Behold the handmaid of the Lord.
R. Be it done unto me according to thy word.
Hail Mary, etc.

V. And the Word was made Flesh.
R. And dwelt among us.
Hail Mary, etc.

V. Pray for us, O holy Mother of God.
R. That we may be made worthy of the promises of Christ.

LET US PRAY

Pour forth, we beseech Thee, O Lord,
Thy grace into our hearts,
that we to whom the Incarnation of Christ Thy Son
was made known by the message of an angel,
may by His Passion and Cross
be brought to the glory of His Resurrection.
Through the same Christ Our Lord. Amen.

Jews are called to prayer by the sounding of the shofar—a ram's horn. It is the only Hebrew cultural instrument to have survived until now. Two different forms of shofar were used in the temple in Jerusalem: one made of ibex horn, its bell ornamented with gold, was sounded at New Year and during the Yovel Days; and one made of ram's horn, with silver ornamentation, was sounded on fast days. Today the use of the shofar is restricted to New Year (Rosh Hashanah) and the Day of Atonement (Yom Kippur).

The Muslim call to prayer is the Azan. The muezzin, a man appointed to call to prayer, climbs the mosque's minaret, and he calls in all directions, "Hasten to prayer."

The Call to Prayer

1 *Allahu Akbar, Allahu Akbar (repeated)*
—Allah is Great, Allah is Great

2 *Ash-hadu al-la Ilaha ill Allah, Ash-hadu al-la Ilaha ill Allah*
—I bear witness that there is no divinity but Allah

3 *Ash-hadu anna Muhammadan Rasulullaah, Ash-hadu anna Muhammadan Rasulullaah*
—I bear witness that Muhammad is Allah's Messenger

4 *Hayya la-s-saleah, Hayya la-s-saleah*
—Hasten to the prayer, Hasten to the prayer

5 *Hayya la-l-faleah, Hayya la-l-faleah*
—Hasten to real success, Hasten to real success

6 *Allahu Akbar, Allahu Akbar*
—Allah is Great, Allah is Great

7 *La Ilaha ill Allah*
—There is no divinity but Allah

Azan is now completed.

Bells are also found throughout Asia in connection with prayer. Today Tibetan bells and singing bowls have become popular in the West. These bells and bowls have a very long "singing" time, which can sooth the mind and initiate one into a state of quiet and prayer. In Zen schools a hollow wooden fish is struck with a wooden hammer to summon the people to meditation.

Drugs

Psychoactive substances have a long association with prayer among the world's peoples. We in the West with our prejudice against drugs are liable to blind ourselves to this association. But even today Christians and Jews place wine at the center of their celebrations: Christians in the Eucharist and Jews in the Sabbath and holy day meals.

The earliest Indians sang the praises of Soma, which they considered the food of the gods. We do not know what this Soma actually was. Some say it could have been a psychedelic mushroom.

The Soma juice pours,
pure, kindly,
bringing visible fullness.

For you the winds blow,
full of love;
for you the rivers flow.
They embrace, Soma, your greatness.

Surge, O Soma, may strength
gather from all sides within you!
You are the central point of all power!

O Great One,
we desire your friendship,
O Drop, mighty defender.

Rig Veda IX 31

Some Native American peoples used the psychedelic peyote to induce visions of the beyond. And tobacco was originally a sacred substance among these peoples and used only in their sacred ceremonies before it was appropriated by Westerners.

exploring a great spiritual practice

chaptersix

The Arts of Prayer

Visual Arts

Sacred art is found throughout the world. We have always attempted to depict our encounter with the sacred in visible form. Indeed, art originated with this sacred mission. Secular art is a modern invention. We know the first art—those wonderful drawings on the caves of southern France—was sacred even if we still do not know its purpose.

Art attempts to visualize the God. Indian art witnesses to the abundance of our religious imagination. Sacred art never calls attention to the artist. The idea of the artist creator—again an image of God—is a modern Western invention. The first time an artist put his signature to his work was a turning point in the history of art.

In the West the idea of God's sheer transcendence over all attempts to visualize was dominant, so in the Judeo-Christian-Muslim tradition the depiction of God visually has always been controversial. Judaism is marked by its aversion to idolatry. The first commandment states, "You shall not make for yourself any graven image." When Moses comes down from the mountain with the Law and finds that the people have made a sacred calf to worship, he smashes the holy tablets to the ground. When you enter a synagogue today you will not find any images there in obedience to this law not to attempt to visualize God.

Christianity also struggled with images in allegiance to this commandment. The Eastern and Western churches were wracked by the Iconoclastic Controversy. Following this debate, the Eastern churches embraced the formalized icon as a door to the holy and the Western church approved of sacred art and statues.

The icon holds a central place in Eastern Christian churches. Icons are holy pictures which are believed to allow the worshipper to meet the holy. They are painted in a very formal way.

Indeed all religious art was originally iconic. It is not meant to be realistic or natural.

Icons in the Eastern church represent the saints present in the Kingdom of God. When the liturgy is celebrated the church on earth and the church in heaven are united.

Today, icons have become quite popular in the West and many modern spiritual mentors such as Martin Luther King, Jr. and Mother Teresa can be found depicted. The only question here is does this person speak to you of God. Does their image and what they stand for help you to approach the divine?

The Western church embraced a more natural form of holy art in her images and statues. But the Protestant reformation raised the issue again. Protestants destroyed many of the pictures and statues as idolatrous. Today Protestant churches still veer toward a suspicion of the visual arts. Instead they have embraced the arts of the word and of music to mediate the divine. The Catholic Church addressed the crisis in the Counter–Reformation, which led to the brilliance of Baroque Rome where stone and paint proclaim the infinite glory of God.

The idea of a religious art that is not a part of the sacred world is unique to the modern West. With the emergence of the Western Renaissance, art detached itself from the church and, while it could still celebrate the holy, was first and foremost a creation of the secular artist. So the great religious examples of art from our celebrated artists—Dürer, Bellini, Michelangelo, Caravaggio, Rembrandt—the whole glorious company produced their art not for worship but for inspiration and admiration.

This is the art we find throughout Western Christianity where it indeed may still be used in a religious way—for example, hung in churches—but not iconic like the traditional art of old whether it be statues or icons. Or might we say that some of these images have attained the status of modern icons. Consider the modern image of the laughing Jesus, which has become part of the prayer life of millions.

Statues have been at the very center of the West's struggle with representing God. The statue, being three dimensional, is even more likely than a mere painting to be mistaken for God. The prophet Isaiah speaks of the statues of the gods which are mere stone as opposed to the living God of Israel who of course can be represented by nothing in His Creation. So there are no statues in the Jewish world. Yes, there are menorahs and other objects for prayer but there are no attempts to depict the divine in stone or wood.

Protestantism and Islam continue this anti-idolatrous theme. In Eastern Christianity only the icon is allowed—statues are forbidden. Only the catholic traditions make a place for statues. But with the consciousness of idolatry so prominent, catholicism has had to apologize and emphasize that it is not engaging in idol worship.

Actually, today the question of idolatry should be a moot issue. The worshipper does not believe that the statue is the divinity. It is a mere representation of the divine. The statue simply exists to give a form to the object of prayer. Every spiritual tradition emphasizes that the divine cannot be represented or captured in any created material.

The debate surrounding statues raises the issues of praying to many gods or of praying to saints or mentors as though they were gods. Hinduism with its pantheon of gods is the focus of the first question. Does a Hindu believe in many gods? No. Rather these images of god Brahma, Shiva, Vishnu, and the others are really but windows into the God beyond all images and thought.

The gods are like a sacrament of God—they mediate an aspect of the All. They are not gods, but, to use a metaphor from another tradition, they are like fingers pointing toward God. Do not mistake the image for that which it points towards.

Let us take an example from the West. In Catholicism there is a statue and a cult of the Sacred Heart of Jesus. You can recognize the statue because the figure of Jesus has a heart on his chest to which he points. There are of course other images of Jesus—the infant in his mother's arms, and the crucified one on the cross are the two most popular.

When a person prays with the Sacred Heart they are narrowing their prayer to one aspect of Jesus—his infinite mercy and compassion for the world. The statue helps the worshipper to focus upon that aspect of His infinite mercy.

When the person then places themselves before the Madonna and Child they are focusing upon another aspect of the divine. The statues are mediating certain aspects of the divine. They themselves are not the divine and they do not encompass all the qualities of the divine. That is impossible.

Further, Catholicism supports the cult of the saints. Are Catholics praying to the saints? Are they guilty of making the saints gods? No. A saint—and there are saints in every tradition—is a spiritual hero.

Like all heroes they serve for our emulation. So we admire their qualities, which are indeed aspects of God that shine especially clearly through them—for example, we admire and wish to emulate St. Paul's fervor for the gospel. The saints are human beings like ourselves. They are our brothers and sisters. They can help us approach God. But they are never an end in themselves.

The spiritualities of the East have an abundance of statues of gods and goddesses. And Buddhism, which claims to be agnostic about God, has statues not only of the Buddha himself but of aspects of the teaching.

One of the favorite images throughout Buddhist East Asia is Kuan Yin, also known as the male bodhisattva Avalokiteshavra. When the Buddha spoke of enlightenment and of the difficulty of attaining it, his disciple Avalokiteshavra was moved to tears. And from one of his tears the goddess Tara was born. Her compassionate nature led the first Christian missionaries to Tibet to confuse her with their own Virgin

Mary, and indeed both do manifest the same qualities of the divine.

The mandala is a sacred figure found throughout the world's spiritualities. Today it is more well known from the Hindu and Buddhist traditions. But Christian mandalas also appear in the halos placed behind saints, and in the rose windows of Gothic cathedrals. The psychologist Carl Jung even saw the modern phenomenon of flying saucers as a contemporary manifestation of the mandala.

The mandala by its round shape provides an image of reality. In the Tibetan tradition the student meditates upon an intricate mandala to break through to the Real. Each tiny part of the mandala must be visualized. The student longs to see the world as mandala and to hear it as mantra.

For special occasions Tibetan monks will also create an elaborate sand mandala. Such a mandala takes days to build. Then at the completion it is swept away to honor the impermanence of all.

The Navajo have created the art of sand painting. There is one kind of sand painting that is for artistic expression. But another kind belongs to the healing or blessing ceremony conducted by a medicine man. The painting is a place where the gods come and go.

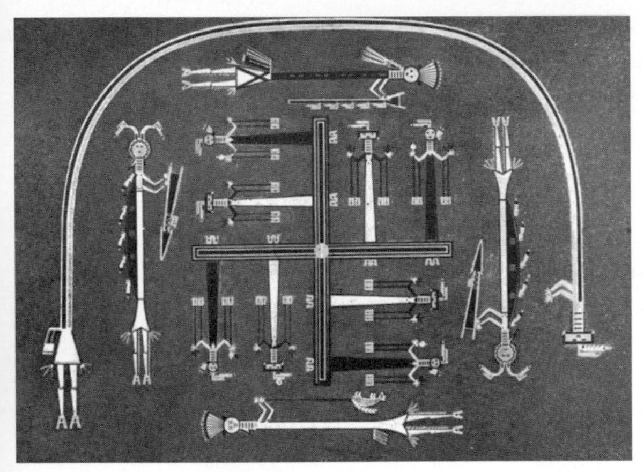

The painting is a key element of the healing ceremony that lasts from two to nine days. It is meant to restore balance, which is a crucial element of Navajo spirituality. The painting is created in one day and then destroyed that night. These paintings are seldom viewed by outsiders.

Tattoos and jewelry have a noble part in the world of prayer. Both were originally part of our prayer world and then degenerated into a secular practice. The tattoo marks the body for God and shows God's symbols. Jewelry does so by bringing precious metals and stones into the service of God.

Today we still see religious jewelry—the most obvious is the Christian cross. The question is whether it is indeed worn for religious or secular reasons.

Both the tattoo and jewelry mark the wearer as belonging to God. They proclaim one's faith to the world. Many spiritualities, including the Christian, emphasize proclaiming one's faith so that others may have a chance to share it.

If you do choose to wear an emblem of faith, make its putting on and taking off into an intentional and prayerful act. What does it mean for me to don this symbol? What does it mean for me to take it off? How did I honor its meaning in my life today?

Relics are remains of holy people or places used in prayer to bring the worshipper into contact with that holiness. In the West they are found in the catholic traditions. The remains of saints are placed in special containers called reliquaries. Then they are placed in shrines and in churches where they become a focus of prayer for their followers.

The giant stupas of Buddhism began as reliquaries containing the remains of Buddha and then developed as a focus for prayer without the remains. Today they are often filled with sacred mantras which, like the original bones, bring the worshipper close to the Real.

It is easy to see how the use of relics could degenerate into superstition and fraud. The medieval monasteries created a practice known as "sacra rapta"—sacred theft—whereby they would steal the relics from other monasteries and reap the material benefits from credulous pilgrims. As the stupa reminds us, the relic like everything else in this world is passing and empty; its only importance is to point us to the Real—to God.

Look at your own spiritual journey. You probably do not have a relic of a saint, but you might have a holy object passed down to you from a parent or teacher that can serve as your own relic. A picture will serve. Is there someone who has shown the face of God for you? Something that opens up for you the way to God? Consider placing this "relic" upon your altar.

Music

Like art, music was originally totally in the service of religion. And all ritual was sung. The modern worship service, which employs the spoken rather than the sung word, is a degeneration.

Look in the Bible's Book of Psalms and you will notice directions for how to sing the psalm at the beginning. Unfortunately we do not possess these ancient melodies today. But the chants of the synagogue are their modern descendants.

I pray and I sing. And sometimes my prayer is my singing.
Bobby McFerrin

The early Christian church sang the psalms. They are chanted to this day in many monasteries and convents. Gregorian Chant, so called after Pope Gregory V who formalized it, remains the official music of the Roman Catholic Church today. The chant was developed to replace the original melodies as they were forgotten. Some of the melodies came from popular songs of the day.

Gregorian chant has become popular through numerous recordings, and as such it can be an aid to prayer. But it is important to remember that originally chant was not something to be listened to passively, but something to be actively entered into. Make sure you keep yourself as the central actor in your prayer. Don't expect these aids to do it for you. Instead of listening to the chant, learn it and chant along with the music.

The Christian East also has a rich history of chant quite different from the West. Gregorian chant has no harmony. It is just one line of music. Orthodox chant, on the other hand, is harmonic and quite rich.

Who sings, prays twice.

St. Benedict

Protestant Christianity has given us the hymn, another form of prayer. Martin Luther wrote hundreds of hymns—the most famous is "A Mighty Fortress is Our God." In England Methodism put the hymn at the center of its spirituality and graced the church with such beloved hymns from the Wesleys as "The Church's One Foundation" and "Love Divine All Love Excelling." In America a former slave trader wrote one of the most beloved hymns—"Amazing Grace." Again like all religious music hymns are meant to be sung by the worshipper. They are music for everyone to sing—not just the professionals.

Precious Lord, take my hand. Lead me on. Let me stand. I am tired. I am weak. I am worn. Through the storm, Through the night, Lead me on to the light. Take my hand, precious Lord, and lead me home.

African American spiritual

So we come to a final category of sacred music—at least in the West—performance music. This may be music originally meant to accompany worship such as the organ and choral works of J.S. Bach. Later it developed into music not for the church but for the concert hall—the oratorios of Handel such as the Messiah and ultimately the "Resurrection" Symphony of Gustav Mahler. Here the composers translate their spiritual experiences into music. And we, as listeners, allow them to usher us into their experience of the divine.

EXERCISE

You may wish to allow a musical genius to introduce you to their experience of God. Of course J. S. Bach should be at the top of the list. His masterwork—the Mass in B Minor—or his organ works such as the Toccata and Fugue in D Minor are good places to begin. Beethoven conquers the spiritual heights in both his Ninth Symphony and his Missa Solemnis. Anton Bruckner, a lowly country church organist all his life, managed to capture his experience in his monumental symphonies where he often found God in nature—try his Fourth Symphony. Gustav Mahler brings this tradition to its apex in his epic symphonies including the abovementioned Symphony No. 2 in C Minor, the "Resurrection" Symphony. The French Catholic mystic Olivier Messiaen used birdsong and Hindu rhythms to chant to God. For an introduction try his final work, Eclairs sur l'au delá (Illuminations from the Beyond).

With any of these pieces find some time and a place where you will not be interrupted. You may want to use good headphones to bring you even closer to the music. Read any material the composer may have left to guide you. Then take a few moments to relax yourself. Close your eyes and allow the composer to share his experience.

Dance

Like art and music, in the beginning all dance was sacred. Imagine the medieval celebration where to begin the sacred liturgy the bishop danced down the aisle with his deacons. Our shock at such an image signals our alienation from our bodies. In the degenerate spiritualities of the West the body was regarded as lower if not dirty and sinful.

The Whirling Dervishes are part of a Sufi order founded by the great poet Rumi. The dervishes wear a long white robe and a white hat. They form a circle and begin slowly twirling, gradually picking up speed. They hold one hand up to God and one hand down to the earth. As they twirl they move around the circle. The dance is designed to bring one into one's center and into contact with God.

Whirling is not the exclusive reserve of the Sufis. As children we all twirled. It induces a special state of consciousness. We twirled until we were shamed out of it and became respectable adults. But try it again as a prayer. How does twirling bring you into your center?

A white man, Edward Curtis, was responsible for bringing news of the Hopi Rain Dance to the Western world. It is also known as the Snake Dance since the Hopis believe that snakes have the power to bring rain from the gods.

The rain dance is not unique. Our ancestors would have always included dance in their rituals and ceremonies. Like the loss of singing, the disappearance of dancing from our prayer is a further sign of our impoverishment as modern people.

exploring a great spiritual practice

chapterseven

The Words of Prayer

Although not absolutely essential, language is usually connected with prayer. And the language associated with prayer is considered sacred. Language's roots are in the sacred and still today we see evidence of the sacredness of language in many traditions.

Words of Power

In the Judeo-Christian tradition Adam, the first man, gives names to the animals. That naming gives him power over them. And since names are sacred the name of God in Israel must not be spoken except by the high priest on the holiest day in the temple. This is the reason for not taking the name of God in vain. It is holy. It has power. It is not ordinary.

For the Christian the tradition of the sacred name continues in the Jesus prayer. His name, which contains the name of God, has the power to transform the pray-er.

The practice of the Jesus Prayer is simple.
Stand before the Lord with the attention in the heart,
and call to Him:
"Lord Jesus Christ, Son of God, have mercy on me!"
The essential part of this is not in the words,
but in faith and contrition,
and self-surrender to the Lord.
With these feelings one can stand before the Lord
even without any words,
and it will still be prayer.

Theophan the Recluse

We see this same reverence for the word in Eastern traditions where the archetypal sound is OM. There too developed the science of the mantra. These words of power, when prayed, transform the one praying. In Tibetan Buddhism the most popular mantra is "Om mani padme hum." This phrase does not mean anything. Each of the words has meanings but the importance lies not in the meaning but in the sound itself.

Common Mantras

OM—the primordial sound
Hindu

Om mani padme hum—no real translation exists
Buddhist

Hallelujah!—Praise be to God
Jewish

Jesus
Christian

There is no God but Allah, and Mohammed is his messenger.
La ilaha ill-llah, Muhammad-un Rasulu-llah
Muslim

One
Relaxation response (Secular Spirituality)

Islam also knows the truth of the power held in a word, as shown in the following Sufi story.

A spiritual teacher was rowing a boat along a lake shore. He heard someone chanting the word, "Alleluia."

Ah, thought the teacher, they are chanting the most powerful prayer. They say that if you chant it properly all kinds of powers will be given to you. Now I have never experienced those powers, but I do know that the teachers all say you must chant the word as Al-LE-lu-ia and this poor student is chanting Al-le-LU-ia. I should help him.

So the teacher beached his boat and entered the student's hut. He told the student that the practice of the chant granted wonderful powers.

But he had also heard that the chant was properly sung as Al-LE-lu-ia. The student was very grateful for this teaching. And as the teacher left and returned to his boat he heard the student chanting, Al-LE-lu-ia. The teacher felt very good that he had helped this student. But as he drifted out into the lake again he heard the chant change. Now the student was back to his old ways, chanting Al-le-LU-ia. Ah, the depths of human sinfulness and ignorance, sighed the teacher.

A few minutes later a touch to his shoulder startled him. He looked around and saw the student walking on the water.

"I'm sorry, great teacher, but could you teach me the correct chant again?"

Sacred Languages

Language itself is sacred and holy. Most spiritual traditions impart to their founding language a place of honor. For the Hindus it is Sanskrit. For Theravada Buddhists it is Pali—the language of the early Buddhist communities. For Tibetan Buddhists the mantras are in Sanskrit although the scriptures have been translated into Tibetan.

For Jews Hebrew remains the language of God. For Christians it may be Greek or Latin. And Islam places Arabic as not just a sacred language but the language God speaks. To be a true Muslim one must learn this sacred tongue.

Study of the sacred language often goes beyond the mere attempt to understand it. Jewish Kabbala finds hidden meanings within the Hebrew Biblical text. And the Sufis do the same for the Qur'an. Obviously these studies are open only to a few and involve a whole lifetime of devotion and study. The current popularization of Kabbala by Hollywood and rock stars is quite controversial.

Finally prayer can ask for a special kind of language, an archaic language. As you will have noticed, a number of prayers in this book use the old English second person—"thou" for "you." There have been fights over language in a number of Christian churches as the managing bodies have attempted to use more contemporary English. Episcopalians have fought over the new Book of Common Prayer. Roman Catholics at first modernized the Lord's Prayer but soon resorted to the traditional form.

Translations of the scriptures have shared in this cultural battle. Should the Word of God sound like today's newspaper or should it be formal and a trifle old fashioned? What is the proper language of prayer? The King James Version of the Bible survives today as much for its "language of God" as for theological reasons.

The Written Word

There are prayer books and then there are Prayer Books. For Jews and Christians the Book of Psalms provide the official prayers of their religion. These psalms (or songs or prayers) were composed over hundreds of years and they give voice to whatever a person may want to take to God in prayer.

There are prayers of praise and thanksgiving. Prayers of petition. Prayers asking forgiveness and penance. Even prayers asking for the downfall and destruction of enemies, which we moderns may find distasteful.

While some of these, such as the Twenty-third Psalm, have become beloved and have served for thousands of years to give voice to our prayers, others are not easy to enter into.

When a Jew or Christian prays these psalms he or she does so as a member of the People of God. "I may not be suffering at this time but some of my brothers and sisters are and I will pray these words in their name." This idea of being a part of a larger body may be difficult for modern people but our failure to do so deprives us of a rich part of being a spiritual person.

No man is an island,
entire of itself. . . .
Any man's death diminishes me,
because I am involved in mankind;
and therefore never send to know
for whom the bell tolls;
it tolls for thee.

"Meditation 17," John Donne

Many people today journal as a way of praying. This way of prayer goes back to St. Augustine in the West. In his Confessions he told God his life story. We might also with a stretch of the imagination see Dante's Divine Comedy as using writing to foster his own conversion. Throughout the ages people have used the journal to examine their spiritual life.

Today the primary guide to spiritual journaling is the psychologist Ira Progoff. In his Intensive Journal program, he sets up the journal using many different sections such as life story, the key people in life, the key events, and God.

The heart of the process is the dialogue that can take place between yourself and people, events, almost anything in your life. For the dialogue the person enters a peaceful and receptive state and then begins writing something to the object of the dialogue. Then in silence he or she awaits a response from the other. There is no judging or censoring of what comes up. With time and practice this dialoguing can open a person to his or her own depths as well as the depths of God.

The Dialogue Journal is only one form of journaling. Especially at the beginning of a prayer journey, it would be helpful to keep a journal. What to place there? First, what is happening in your life? How are you praying? What is happening in the prayer? Do you feel fulfilled? Frustrated? Frightened? Hopeful? What kinds of prayer are you engaging in? What is your practice of public worship, if any? What are

your thoughts regarding the sermon or homily? What are your thoughts regarding spiritual books you are reading? What are your feelings as you approach spiritual holidays such as Christmas or Passover?

As you write, use the present tense rather than the past. Write from a place of rest and openness. Before writing, take a little time to calm yourself. Stretch a little. Take three or more deep breaths. Let the tensions and thoughts flow out with the out breath. Take your time. When you are calm and relaxed you can begin journaling.

Begin by describing your current state. What is happening? Who are the characters in this moment of your life? What are the events? How do you feel about this moment? What are your emotions? Thoughts? Concerns? Bring it to God in your words. Don't worry about how best to say it. You are not writing for anyone else to read. The writing is merely a vehicle to lead you into prayer. When you speak to God and write it down, wait a few moments in silence. Then write whatever comes up. Do not censor anything. Do not judge. Don't worry about whether this is really God or not. Simply enter into the process.

Lectio divina (sacred reading) comes from the monks in the early days of Christianity. It is commonly attributed to St. Benedict, the founder of Western monasticism. Here the pray-er focuses upon the words of a holy book. But he or she reads in a very different way from normal. Lectio divina is a very contemplative way of reading. You may only cover a few verses or even words of scripture in one session. The traditional instructions ask the pray-er to ruminate upon the words as a cow chews her cud.

Dwell on each word. What does it mean to you? Remain with it in silence. Allow yourself to free associate. Where does your prayer take you? Don't worry about falling off topic. That may happen, but if you curb yourself in too much you limit God's ability to speak to you. How has this word appeared in your spiritual history? When you are ready, move on to the next word. Explore it. Also explore how it relates to the preceding word. There should be no goal in this reading. No need to reach the end of the passage. Be in the present. Allow the scriptures to reveal themselves to you. Allow God to speak to you through God's holy Word.

Pray the Lord's Prayer through, and then take one of the phrases. Spend a few moments reflecting on that phrase, for example, imagining what it means for God's Kingdom to come, or how we forgive those who sin against us. Then use these thoughts for further prayer, finally coming back to pray through the Lord's Prayer again.

Speaking in Tongues

Charismatic Christians practice what they call "speaking in tongues" or "glossolalia." They trace this prayer back to the New Testament, the story of the descent of the Holy Spirit upon the disciples at Pentecost. As the tongues of fire descended upon these disciples they began to speak so that all the people assembled in Jerusalem could hear the Good News of Jesus' resurrection in their own languages.

For the most part today charismatics do not speak known tongues but rather through ecstatic utterance they praise God. Associated with the speaking in tongues is the gift of prophecy: the pray-er speaks in tongues and another charismatic translates the utterance for the congregation. These are thought to be gifts of the Holy Spirit bestowed upon the believer. They are not something the pray-er has control over. Rather the pray-er is caught up in the Spirit who speaks through him or her.

exploring a great spiritual practice

chaptereight

The Body in Prayer

I recognize you are the temple
in which my spirit and creative energy dwell.
I have created you from my need
to have my spirit manifested on earth
so that I may have this time to learn and grow.
I offer you this food so that you may continue
to sustain my creative energy, my spirit, my soul.
I offer this food to you with love,
and a sincere desire for you to remain free
from disease and
disharmony.
I accept you as my own creation.
I need you.
I love you.

"Affirmation to My Body," Hindu

Westerners have not paid much attention to the body in prayer. In fact some of our prayer postures can even be counterproductive to the best prayer. So let us now explore the various ways in which our bodies can enter into prayer, besides through dance, which we have already covered.

Prayer Postures

In the West kneeling is the most accepted posture of prayer. So it is all the more interesting that kneeling only entered into prayer in the Middle Ages. It was appropriated from court life where one would kneel in homage to one's superiors.

Today it is often regarded as the posture of basic prayer. Certainly kneeling does signal your relationship to God. It is a posture of beseeching. It emphasizes the gulf between humanity and God. God is infinitely superior. This posture certainly works on our human pride and many of us need to fall on our knees to remind ourselves of our limitations.

You may have bad associations with kneeling, however. And if you do, do not let kneeling be an obstacle to your prayer. There are many other postures, as we shall see.

Actually, the original posture of Christian prayer was standing. Standing is a way of proclaiming the resurrection of Jesus through bodily posture. And today Christians still stand in different parts of their worship services. However, few use it in their private prayer.

Standing is also used in Taoist martial arts as a posture for meditation. Here the emphasis is upon learning to assume the posture so that one is able to persevere for long periods of time. The posture is not primarily for prayer or more properly meditation, but for developing physical strength and perseverance.

One can pray in any posture and sitting is a perfectly acceptable prayer posture. The danger in sitting is that you might fall asleep as you wouldn't if kneeling or standing. Sitting is also a more passive posture than kneeling or standing.

The important thing with all of these postures is not the posture itself, but what enables you to pray. Try each of these postures for a while. Let them teach you about prayer.

Some schools of Buddhism offer a six-pointed posture, which makes sitting a productive means of prayer. If you can, you may wish to assume one of the Eastern postures—the half or even the full lotus. But since most of us Westerners are used to chairs we will assume a sitting posture in a chair.

First, put your feet on the ground. Do not cross your legs as this makes you unstable. Only one of your buttocks will be on the seat. But if you place both feet on the floor you ground and stabilize yourself. Try crossing your legs and then put both feet on the floor. Feel the difference. This is no mystery—it is simple common sense. Use a hard chair. A soft chair is likely to be too comfortable and lead to sleep or at least inattention.

Second, sit with your seat a few inches out from the back of the chair. This way if you do nod off you will wake yourself as you fall back against the chair.

Third, place your hands where they are relaxed. You can place your palms over your knees. Or you can use a gesture or mudra, which we will explore later in this chapter. The key thing is to choose a gesture and stick with it. Then if you find your hands wandering during prayer you know where to put them back.

Fourth, sit with your back straight but not rigid. You want to assume a posture that is midway between tension and relaxation. Too tense and God cannot approach you. Too relaxed and you fall asleep.

Fifth, open your mouth slightly. Try to breathe equally between your nose and mouth. What are you going to do with your tongue? Let the tip gently touch the ridge just above your front teeth.

And sixth, we move up to your eyes. If you are going to be distracted, you probably should close your eyes. If that is not a problem allow your eyes to be open. Gaze, don't stare. Assume the look of a mother gazing at her child.

We do not have to remain still or sitting for prayer. Walking is found throughout the world of prayer. Buddhists pray by circumambulating the stupa. Catholics pray by walking up and down their churches while meditating upon the Stations of the Cross—fifteen moments from Jesus' Passion.

If you have problems sitting down for extended periods of time, try walking prayer instead. First, find a good place for a walk. Find a quiet place. You may want to walk in a place of natural beauty. At the very least walk where there is no vehicular traffic and noise.

Take a moment or two to calm and center yourself. Take a couple of long deep breaths. When you are centered, stand up and begin to walk.

Walk slowly. You can walk around in a small circle or back and forth in a line—that is all you need. You may want to synchronize your walk with your breath. Walk with awareness. And when you are ready, open your heart to

God. As you walk be mindful of your body. Draw your awareness inward. Open yourself to the God within.

Your prayer place may not be in one single place on earth. We are mobile creatures. You may be on a journey. Indeed we are all of us on journeys. This journey reveals the story of our life.

But what if the journey itself is the prayer? Then you are on pilgrimage—a sacred journey that will bring you closer to the divine. The pilgrim hopes to come close to the divine by leaving ordinary life behind and setting off to discover his or her soul.

The goal is often some holy place. And the journey, although it may be made alone, is best done in company with other pilgrims. Through the common experience all are renewed and return to their homes ready to share their stories with those left behind and so include them in the renewal as well.

The Stations of the Cross mentioned previously grew out of the medieval Christian pilgrimage to the Holy Land. And the goal of the journey would inevitably be to walk the way of Jesus' last hours on earth. Naturally such a pilgrimage could only be undertaken by a few. And it cost years of your life and thousands of dangers. The Christian who could not afford to make the actual pilgrimage could participate vicariously by making the Stations.

Each Muslim as part of the five pillars of their faith is required if at all possible to make the Hajj once in a lifetime. This is a pilgrimage to the holy city of Mecca where the pilgrims eventually come to the Kaaba and circle it. The Hajj, because all real pilgrimage takes us out of our routines, can be a life transforming experience.

The labyrinth makes an excellent symbol of our spiritual journey. It is not a maze or puzzle. Caught in a maze, you try to find your way out. The labyrinth is a tool for prayer. There is only one path; there are no dead ends or wrong turns. You begin on the edge and walk to the center, then you turn around and follow the path out to the edge again.

Labyrinth is a form of pilgrimage. People take pilgrimages as a means of spiritual renewal. The pilgrimage itself is holy and sacred. The journey will change us, transform us, renew us. So the labyrinth is a symbol of that sacred journey.

Labyrinths have been around for over four thousand years in almost every spiritual tradition. They are found in old cathedrals, in gardens. Today they are again being built as vehicles for self exploration and growth. First, you must find a labyrinth. A little work on the computer may help you find one nearby.

There are many approaches to the labyrinth. Today, labyrinths are being used for reflection, meditation, prayer, and comfort. Each person's walk is personal. How one walks and what one receives differs. Some use the walk to clear the mind and center. Others bring a question or concern. As you walk to the center bring your hopes, desires, and prayers to God.

The time in the center can be used for receiving, reflecting, meditating, or praying, as well as discovering our own sacred inner space.

What each person receives may be integrated on the walk out. How will you use what you have received in your life? Your walk may be a healing and very profound experience or it may be just a pleasant walk. Each time is different.

Clear your mind and become aware of your breathing.

Find the pace your body wants to go.

Walking toward the center, let the path quiet your mind.

From the entrance to the goal is the path of shedding or "letting go."

Release and empty yourself of worries and concerns.

When you reach the center,
take time for illumination,
reflection,
or meditation.

At the center there is illumination, insight, clarity, and focus. Here you are in a receptive, prayerful, meditative mood.

As you walk back out,
be strengthened for your return into the world.

The path out is that of becoming grounded and integrating the insight.

It is being energized and making what was received manifest in the world.

"Meditation on the Labyrinth"

Lying down is not a notable posture for prayer. And it is problematic because many of us will fall asleep. But it has been used. One of the classic statues of Buddha finds him reclining. And St. Ignatius of Loyola prayed lying down. Of course he laid on a hard floor, not a soft bed. If falling asleep is not a problem, you might want to try praying lying down. It definitely relaxes you and makes you more open to God.

Prayer Gestures

What to do with your hands in prayer? It is first of all a practical concern. If we do not have a position for our hands they are likely to wander all over the place. But more than that, a gesture becomes an enfleshed prayer. And making the gesture ushers us into the world of prayer.

In the East prayer gestures are called mudras. "Mudra" means sign or seal and refers not only to sacred hand gestures but to whole body postures that elicit an inner state and symbolize a particular meaning. There are many; more than can be covered here. We will limit ourselves to two of the most popular mudras.

For the Anjali mudra you either sit or stand and draw both your palms together at your heart. This is very similar to the usual Western gesture—the praying hands. It is a gesture of offering and is often used to greet people and gods. The pray-er may add the word, "Namaste"—"I bow to the divinity within you from the divinity within me."

For the Meditation mudra, in a sitting posture place the right hand over the left palm with the tips of both thumbs touching lightly. Your hands rest palms up in your lap. The right hand symbolizes enlightenment; the left the world of appearance (illusions). The mudra represents the triumph of the world of enlightenment over the world of illusions.

Catholic Christians trace the sign of the cross upon their bodies as a sign of blessing. They will often do this upon entering a church where they will use holy water to recall their baptism. They do it as well to begin prayer.

To make the sign of the cross take your right hand, join the thumb, index, and middle finger together. The three fingers represent the Holy Trinity, the two fingers the dual nature of Christ—human and divine. Now you may dip your finger in holy water if you want. Make the sign by touching your forehead and say, "In the name of the Father." Touch your stomach and say, "And of the Son." And touch your left and right shoulders saying, "And of the Holy Spirit." Some now kiss the three fingers. Orthodox Christians make broader movements than Western Christians and they go from right to left shoulders.

The believer also makes the sign of the cross upon genuflecting to honor the presence of God. Genuflect toward the tabernacle where the Eucharist is reserved or the cross above the altar. To genuflect kneel down upon your right knee.

Bring your two palms together, fingers pointing up. This is the most famous Christian prayer gesture made famous by Dürer's Praying Hands. Like the mudra it brings your being together in your heart, and the fingers point upward toward heaven or God.

Here is a gesture used when Catholics receive Holy Communion but it is perfect for any prayer. Place your hands crossed, palms up. Your thumbs touch lightly. The upturned palms symbolize your receptiveness to God. The crossed hands form a cross—the means of salvation.

Bowing and prostration are also common prayer gestures. They are found more in the East than in the West although some catholic Christians bow rather than genuflect in the presence of the Eucharist. Both are signs of respect and submission.

In some Buddhist schools, particularly in Tibet, prostration is considered a powerful method to purify our past misdeeds or karma. Prostrating gets rid of the obstacles of arrogance and ego and pays homage to the enlightened ones.

For half prostration kneel down and touch both hands and forehead to the ground. For the full prostration stretch out your whole body to the ground.

Practitioners here may use sliding boards or knee pads. The pray-er may do the prostration at one holy site, or go on a one thousand mile pilgrimage, prostrating every second step.

It is important to remember the ultimate teaching of Buddha—all is emptiness. There is no real self. So the one who bows and the one bowed to are both empty by nature. The bodies of yourself and the other are not two.

Salat are the prayers which form the core of a Muslim's daily prayer. They are performed five times—dawn, noon, afternoon, sunset, and bedtime. They may be said alone or with others at a mosque or other gathering place. In a Muslim community there is a call to prayer, the Azan.

First face in the direction of the Kaaba (the first mosque, built by Abraham and his son Ismail) in Mecca.

In the United States this is slightly south of east.

Now perform Ablution. Wash your face, your arms to the elbows, wipe you head with your wet hands, and wash your feet to the ankles.

Now face Mecca and state your intention to enter into Contact prayer.

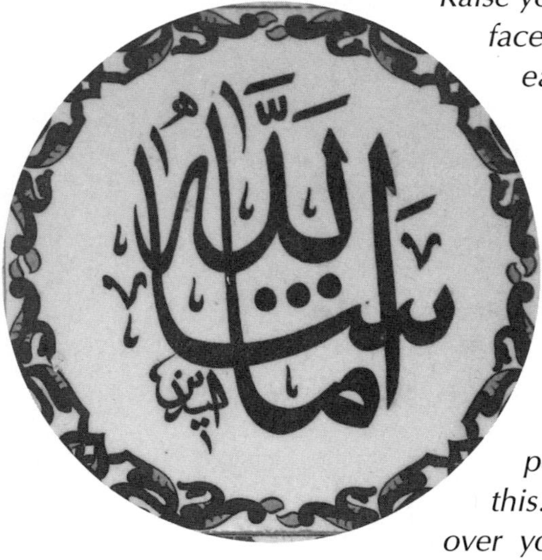

Raise your hands to the sides of your face. Your thumbs touch your ears and your palms face forward. As you raise your hands to your face and then down again to your sides in a continuous motion pray, Allahu Akbar (God is Great).

Bring your hands back to your sides. For the standing posture you may remain like this. Or you may put your hands over your stomach, right hand on top of the left.

Now recite the Opening of the Qur'an. Do this in Arabic even if you do not understand the language. The prayer is in the sounds of Allah speaking to mere mortals.

"The Key"

1. BISMIL LAAHIR RAHMAANIR RAHEEM.
   (In the name of GOD, Most Gracious, Most Merciful.)
2. AL HAMDU LILLAHI RABBIL `AALAMEEN.
   (Praise be to GOD, Lord of the universe.)

3. AR RAHMAANIR RAHEEM.
   (Most Gracious, Most Merciful.)
4. MAALIKI YAWMID DEEN.
   (Master of the Day of Judgment.)
5. EYYAAKA NA`BUDU, WA EYYAAKA NASTA`EEN.
   (You alone we worship; You alone we ask for help.)
6. EH'DENAS SIRAATAL MUSTAQEEM.
   (Guide us in the right path.)
7. SIRAATAL LAZINA AN`AMTA `ALAYHIM; GHAYRIL *MAGHDOOBI `ALAYHIM WALADDAALEEN.*

   (The path of those whom You blessed; not of those who have deserved wrath, nor of the strayers.)

As you move from standing to bowing, pray "Allahu Akbar." Bow from your waist. Keep your knees straight. Place your hands on your knees. Pray "God be glorified."

As you stand, pray "God responds to those who praise Him."

Now fall prostrate and as you go down say, "Allahu Akbar."

As you sit up from the prostrate position, pray "Allahu Akbar." Now prostrate a second time praying "Allahu Akbar." During the second prostration pray "God be glorified." As you stand up pray "Allahu Akbar."

This completes one unit. Each of the prayer times have an assigned number of units. I encourage you to try it for a while. Don't do it once, decide it is too foreign and give it up. Of course at first it will be foreign. But it has held the prayers of billions of people over the centuries. Let it hold yours.

The series of asanas (postures) from Hatha Yoga called the Salute to the Sun form an excellent bodily prayer as well as a way to move from the everyday world into the realm of the sacred. It takes only a minute but provides a full stretch to the body and is an excellent way of centering. In the West today it has been joined to the Lord's Prayer and in the following the appropriate phrases are indicated at the right time if you want to add this prayer to the asana.

In learning this sequence, break it up into the various postures—forward bend, backward leg stretch, plank position, cobra, and so on. Again, it is not important to do the stretch perfectly at first. Do what you can with a gentle exertion. Do not pull the body into a stretch. Rather see how within the posture you can let go of tension and sink into the posture—this is especially the case with the forward bend and the cobra. Do not push or pull, but relax and let go. If it is too much to do the breathing at first, learn the posture and add the breathing later.

Salute to the Sun

Stand up straight, feet together, knees straight but not locked.

Now allow your arms to move out and upwards to the sides as you inhale.

Join the palms over your head and bring the hands down in front of your face in a prayer position as you exhale.

Our Father

Inhaling reach the hands up and over your head again.

Bend just slightly backwards.

Look upwards toward your hands. Do not overdo this stretch.

Who art in heaven

Then return to upright with hands stretching upward.

As you exhale begin to bend forward.

Stretch out with the arms as you bend downwards.

Keep going until your hands touch the ground in front of your legs (or stretch as far down as you can. Then if necessary bend your knees to allow the hands to touch the floor.)

The feet and hands should form a straight line.

Hallowed be thy name

Inhaling stretch your left leg backwards
so that the toes and knee rest on the floor.

At the same time raise your head and feel the stretch all along the back and the leg.

Thy Kingdom come

Exhaling move your right leg back so that it joins the left, at the same time lift your left knee off the floor.

Push up so you are in a triangle position with your buttocks at the apex.

Thy will be done

Inhaling now drop the knees,

On Earth

chin,

As it is

and chest

in heaven

to the floor in that order.

When you are lying on the floor push yourself up into the Cobra asana while holding your breath.

Give us this day our daily bread

To do the Cobra asana:
raise your forehead, nose, chin, neck,
and then shoulders from the floor.

Your hands are still in the same position as when you touched the floor with them.

Try to lift using the back muscles rather than pushing with the hands and arms.

As you lift up look upward with the eyes as far as possible and allow the chin to jut outwards and upwards.

Hold the position for a moment and then come down just the reverse of how you went up.

The forehead should be the last to touch the floor.

During the posture keep the legs together and as relaxed as possible.

It is not important how far you stretch but simply that you extend yourself a little.

Push up again into the triangle posture, hand and toes on the floor, buttocks in the air.

Forgive us our trespasses

Now as you inhale bring the left foot between your hands.

The right leg remains stretched out behind with the knee on the ground.

Again stretch by looking up and feeling the stretch all along the back.

as we forgive those who trespass against us

Then exhaling bring the right leg forward to join the left between the hands.

And lead us not into temptation

Inhaling stretch the arms upwards over the head and once again stretch backwards just a little.

The head follows so that in the extreme position your eyes are looking upwards and a little backwards.

but deliver us from evil.

Exhaling allow the arms to come forward, palms joined together in a prayer position.

As the arms lower in front of the body allow the hands to gently touch the forehead,

For thine is the kingdom,

the mouth,

and the power,

and the heart.

and the glory forever.

Allow the arms to descend until they come to rest at your sides.

Amen.

There are various gestures of blessing found throughout the world. One of the most common is a raised hand—either both hands or the right hand, seldom only the left. Catholic and Orthodox Christians are blessed as the priest makes the sign of the cross with his right hand. Blessing is also done by sprinkling the faithful with holy water. And another gesture of blessing sees the right hand placed upon the bowed head of the one to be blessed.

May it be delightful
my house;
From my **head**
may it be delightful;
To my **feet**
may it be delightful;
Where I **lie**
may it be delightful;
All **above me**
may it be delightful;
All **around me**
may it be
delightful.

Navajo chant

exploring a great spiritual practice

chapternine

The Spirit of Prayer

As we approach the end of our pilgrimage let us consider some of humanity's most honored prayers. These words have nourished and guided people for centuries. They provide a veritable summit of prayer. For us they can be a summing up of what we have learned on our journey.

Gayatri Mantra, Hindu

AUM
Bhuh Bhuvah Svah
Tat Savitur Varenyam
Bhargo Devasya Dheemahi
Dhiyo Yo nah Prachodayat
AUM
We meditate upon the glorious splendor
of the Vivifier divine,
May we receive thy supreme sin-destroying light,
Guide our intellect in the right direction. AUM

This may be the oldest prayer still commonly recited. An example of the mantra is given in verse 3.62.10 of the Rig Veda. The Gayatri is the Mother of the Vedas, the most ancient scriptures of Hinduism. The Skanda Purana claims that nothing in the Vedas is superior to the Gayatri. The name refers to the meter in which the mantra is composed. The translation is only approximate. Like many mantras the meaning is subordinate to the sound of the syllables.

Originally the mantra was just an invocation to the sun to bless all on earth. Over time it came to be regarded as a mystic formula of universal power. It is chanted in the original Sanskrit rather than in a translation for it is believed that the words and sounds themselves have the power to illuminate. The Gayatri inspires wisdom.

That glorious splendor of Savitr (the Sun):
the Sun in the heavens is assuredly Savitr.
He it is who is to be sought by one desirous of the Self.
So it is affirmed by those
who disclose the knowledge of Brahman for us.
May we meditate on the Vivifier divine:
Savitr assuredly is God.
Therefore I meditate on that
which is called his splendor.
So it is affirmed by those who disclose the knowledge of Brahman for us.
May he himself illumine our minds:
Mind assuredly is intelligence.
May he breath it into us.
So it is affirmed by those
who disclose the knowledge of Brahman for us.

Maitri Upanishad

It is chanted at dawn, noon, and dusk as well as other times during the day. It is imparted to a disciple by his teacher. You must be initiated into it. Only then do you have the right to pray it.

Some say it should be prayed at dawn until you see the rising sun, and at sunset until you see the evening star. Some say it must be chanted sixteen times daily by its disciples.

It is believed that by chanting the Gayatri mantra and firmly establishing it in the mind, if you carry on your life and do the work that is ordained for you, your life will be full of happiness.

Refuge Prayer, Buddhist

Homage to Him, the Exalted One,
the Arahant, the All-enlightened One.
To the Buddha I go for refuge.
To the Teaching I go for refuge.
To the Order I go for refuge.

Saying this prayer three times makes one a Buddhist. The prayer takes many different forms throughout the Buddhist world, but everywhere it is the foundation of Buddhist life.

The vow is threefold. First the pray-er goes for refuge to the Buddha. This is the Enlightened One. He discovered the Four

Noble Truths, the Eightfold Path, and the truth of codependent origination. Through this vow the person takes Shakyamuni as his or her primary teacher—the one who can lead all to liberation.

In Mahayana Buddhism, "Buddha" is no longer simply the title of Shakyamuni Buddha, the fifth century BCE teacher. Buddha now refers to enlightenment itself.

The second vow seeks refuge in the Dharma—the teaching of the Buddha. The Buddha himself does not liberate, at least in original Buddhism. The Buddha is a savior only in the sense that he presents the truth which liberates. It is up to the person to actualize his or her liberation by following the teachings. So the Truth becomes the second refuge.

Finally the Buddhist takes refuge in the community—the Sangha. We are not simply individuals. We are part of the human community. We are related to one another. Everything in the universe is related to every other thing.

The Sangha is not simply a group of fellow believers. They help me find liberation and I help them. The Sangha is more than just physical presence. Many Buddhists are hermits, but they too are part of the Sangha. The Sangha preserves the teachings. It provides the support for a person to be a hermit.

In Mahayana Buddhism one takes a further vow—the Bodhisattva Vow, that one will not enter into Nirvana until the last blade of grass is also enlightened. Here one truly recognizes that unless all are enlightened, no one is enlightened.

The passions of delusion are inexhaustible.

I vow to extinguish them all at once.

The number of beings is endless. I vow to help save them all.

The Truth cannot be told. I vow to tell it.

The Way which cannot be followed is unattainable. I vow to attain it.

Bodhisattva Vow

Shema, Jewish

Shema Ysirael, Adonai Eloheinu, Adonai Ekhad.
In an undertone:
Barukh Shem k'vod malkhuto l'olam va-ed
V-ahavta et Adonai Elohecha b-chol l'vavcha u-v-chol naf'sh'cha u-v-chol m'odecha.

Hear, O Israel, the Lord is our God, the Lord is One.
In an undertone:
Blessed be the Name of His glorious kingdom for ever and ever

And you shall love the Lord your God with all your heart
and with all your soul and with all your might.
Deuteronomy 6:4, 5

And these words that I command you today shall be in your heart. And you shall teach them diligently to your children, and you shall speak of them when you sit at home, and when you walk along the way, and when you lie down and when you rise up. And you shall bind them as a sign on your hand, and they shall be for frontlets between your eyes. And you shall write them on the doorposts of your house and on your gates.

Deuteronomy 6:6-9

Known as the Shema after the first word in Hebrew, this is the core prayer of Judaism. It was given along with the Law in the desert where God established Israel as God's people.

Unlike some other religions, Judaism is not universalistic. It is the religion of a specific people—the Jews—who were liberated from slavery in Egypt and given the promised land, the site of present day Israel. God chose the Jews to be his people and to be a sign of God to the nations. So we see that "Israel" is the second word of this prayer. A Jew is first and foremost a member of this chosen group.

The first line of the Shema, "Hear O Israel, the Lord is our God, the Lord is One," is repeated throughout the prayer services. Orthodox Jews will recite their prayers in Hebrew, the sacred language. More liberal Jews pray it in the vernacular.

It is said in the morning blessings, and in the Musaf Amidah of Shabbat and holidays. It is prayed when the Torah is taken out of the Ark on Shabbat and holidays. It is prayed as a bedtime prayer, as part of the deathbed confessional, and at various other times.

The Shema may be said while standing or sitting. The Jews of Israel used to stand to show the Shema's importance and to demonstrate that saying Shema is an act of testifying in God. Testimony in a Jewish court is always given while standing.

The first statement is that God is One. Israel first lived among peoples of many gods. Each people had a pantheon of gods. And each country had its own gods. How did the gods of one people relate to the gods of another? Uncompromising monotheism is Israel's genius. First Israel realized that there is only one God for her and that worship of all other gods is for naught. As her faith developed, Israel discerned that that same God is God of all peoples, not just the Jews. Today we often miss just how radical this breakthrough was. That Christians and Muslims along with Jews today are monotheists is due to the experience of Israel.

Notice the command. It is not "You shall obey" or "You shall fear" or some other word. No, it is a command to love. God demands that we love him with all our heart first. Love is first and foremost of the heart.

The prayer continues with the soul and with strength. We might translate these phrases as the mind—soul—and our will—strength. We are called to love God with all our heart, with our mind, and with our will. Let us love with all our being.

Does your spirituality encompass all of your being? It is just a matter of the heart. Is it only something you read about and study? Does it flow into your outward behavior? Does it make a difference in how you act in the world? Only an integral and integrated spirituality is a true spirituality.

Jesus was an orthodox Jew. When asked the essence of the Law he quotes this prayer and then adds, "And you shall love your neighbor as yourself." This too is a Jewish injunction. Conversely there is nothing in the prayer Jesus taught, the Lord's Prayer, that is specifically Christian. It can be recited by a Jew or a Muslim without violating any part of their faith.

The **Our Father** contains all possible petitions; we cannot conceive of any prayer not already contained in it. It is to prayer what **Christ** is to **humanity**. It is impossible to say it once through, giving the fullest possible attention to each word, without a change, infinitesimal perhaps but real, taking **place in the soul.**

Simone Weil

The Lord's Prayer, Christian

Our Father
Who art in heaven
Hallowed be Thy Name.
Thy Kingdom come.
Thy Will be done
on earth as it is in heaven.
Give us this day our daily bread,
and forgive us our trespasses
as we forgive those who trespass against us.
And lead us not into temptation,
but deliver us from evil.

For thine is the kingdom,
and the power,
and the glory
forever.
Amen.

Our Father who art in heaven

Jesus invites his disciples not only to call God Father but a specific name for Father. He refers to God as "Abba," which is the term of endearment a child uses to speak to their father. It is similar to Papa or Daddy. It shows total intimacy. This is the new revelation. The God of Israel might be called Father, but certainly not Papa.

You might want to spend some time with this name. How does it sit with you? How does it challenge your image of God?

> *Let our whole life as we pray without ceasing say "Our Father, which art in heaven," having its citizenship in no wise upon earth but in every way in the heavens which are God's thrones, inasmuch as the kingdom of God is set up in all those who bear the image of the heavenly and for that reason have become heavenly.*
>
> *On Prayer*, Origen

Jesus not only gives God a name, but he calls us into relationship with God. The Christian enters into that relationship through baptism. Further, this relationship is not primarily one on one. When we pray "Our Father," we are part of a community, of a people.

Grandfather, Great Spirit you have been always,
And before you nothing has been.
There is no one to pray to but you.
The star nations all over the heavens are yours,
And yours are the grasses of the earth.
Grandfather, Great Spirit, fill us with the light.
Teach us to walk the soft earth as relatives to all that live.
Help us, for without you we are nothing.

"Great Spirit Guide Us," Black Elk

"Who art in heaven" refers to the history of God. God is of the heavens, the sky. This heavenly feature of God is almost universal. There are sky gods and earth gods. The sky gods are usually of greater awe. They also tend to be masculine while the earthen deities are feminine.

Being the God of all creation, God is in the heavens—over all that is. We pray to the power that brought into being everything that is and that sustains everything in being from moment to moment.

Hallowed be Thy Name

The Creation babbles to us,
like a child which cannot articulate
what it wants to say;

for it is struggling to utter the one Word,
the Name . . . of God.

St. John of the Cross

To hallow is to sanctify—to make holy. We may be called into intimacy with God but that does not forget God's utter transcendence. So we make God's name holy. We give God praise and thanksgiving. We acknowledge God's total otherness. God is wholly other than any created thing. Moses takes off his shoes in the presence of the burning bush. We must never forget the mystery that is God.

May Your name be holy.

Q. What does this mean?

A. Of course, God's name is holy in and of itself, but by this request, we pray that He will make it holy among us, too.

Q. How does this take place?

A. When God's Word is taught clearly and purely, and when we live holy lives as God's children based upon it. Help us, Heavenly Father, to do this! But anyone who teaches and lives by something other than God's Word defiles God's name among us. Protect us from this, Heavenly Father!

Martin Luther

Thy Kingdom come

The focus of Jesus' ministry was the Kingdom of God—a state of being which leads to our fulfillment and happiness. It is not a place. It has come to be associated with heaven, but that is not entirely true.

Be at peace with your own soul,
then heaven and earth will be at peace with you.
Enter eagerly into the treasure house that is within you,
you will see the things that are in heaven;
for there is but one single entry to them both.
The ladder that leads to the Kingdom
is hidden within your soul. . . .
Dive into yourself, and in your soul you will discover
the stairs by which to ascend.

St. Isaac of Nineveh

The Kingdom can exist right here and now if the person is open to it. Its ultimate name is love. And Jesus often described it in the parables—short stories—which he told.

The kingdom of heaven
is like treasure hidden in a field,
which a man found and covered up;
then in his joy he goes
and sells all that he has and buys that field.

Again, the kingdom of heaven
is like a merchant in search of fine pearls,
who, on finding one pearl of great value,
went and sold all that he had and bought it.
Matthew 13:44-46

Thy Will be done on earth as it is in heaven

The heart of all prayer, when all is said and done, is abiding in the will of God. Jesus at the end of his life as he awaits his crucifixion prays that God may save him from this ordeal. But he ends even that prayer, "Not my will but thy will be done."

Prayer might be described as a school in discovering and doing the will of God. There is nothing else we are asked to do, and ultimately nothing else we can do.

THY WILL BE DONE ON EARTH AS IT IS IN HEAVEN,
so that we may love you with all our heart,
by always having you in mind;
with all our soul,
by always longing for you;
with all our mind,
by determining to seek
your glory in everything;
and with all our strength,
of body and soul,
by lovingly serving you
alone.
May we love our
neighbors as ourselves,
and encourage them all to
love you,
by bearing our share
in the joys and sorrows of
others,
while giving offense to no
one.

St. Francis of Assisi

Give us this day our daily bread

We ask for our daily bread, acknowledging that all we have comes from God. We are creatures. We can do nothing on our own. And that leads us to surrender, and to allow our gracious God to nourish and sustain us.

For the Christian this phrase has further significance inasmuch as it points towards the Eucharist. Jesus becomes our daily food and drink in the Eucharist. Here is the depth of the mystery of God's sustaining power.

We pray that those who lack bread shall have it,
and that those who have it,
shall hunger and thirst for justice
for those who have it not.

Latin American grace

And forgive us our trespasses

All that we ought to have thought
and have not thought,
All that we ought to have said,
and have not said,
All that we ought to have done,
and have not done.

All that we ought not to have thought,
and yet have thought,

All that we ought not to have spoken,
and yet have spoken,
All that we ought not to have done,
and yet have done;
For thoughts, works and works,
pray we, O God, for forgiveness.

Persian prayer

The Kingdom is founded upon the forgiveness of sins. The two pillars of Jesus' ministry were the healing of sickness—even sickness to death—and the forgiving of sins. For the Christian this forgiveness is celebrated in baptism, which washes away all sins and provides a fresh start in life.

For Catholics and Orthodox Christians forgiveness after

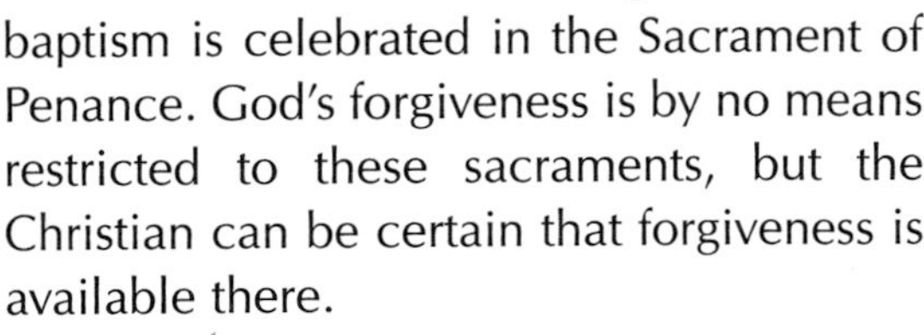

baptism is celebrated in the Sacrament of Penance. God's forgiveness is by no means restricted to these sacraments, but the Christian can be certain that forgiveness is available there.

My Heavenly Father,
I thank You,
through Jesus Christ, Your beloved Son,
that You have protected me, by Your grace.
Forgive, I pray, all my sins
and the evil I have done.

Protect me, by Your grace, tonight.
I put myself in your care,
body and soul and all that I have.
Let Your holy angels be with me,
so that the evil enemy will not gain power over me.
Amen.

"Evening Prayer," Martin Luther

As we forgive those who trespass against us

Jesus comes back to emphasize only this phrase of the prayer. "For if you forgive men their trespasses, your heavenly Father also will forgive you; but if you do not forgive men their trespasses, neither will your Father forgive your trespasses."

God's forgiveness is dependent upon our continuing that forgiveness to the brother or sister who hurts us. This prayer calls us to heroic acts. It is not easy to forgive. It brings up all our fears. It threatens our ego, which we believe is who we truly are. The spiritual path is not easy. It ultimately demands the death of our self and that happens largely through the practice of forgiving sins.

It is the enemy who can truly teach us to practice the virtues of compassion and tolerance.

Dalai Lama

O Allah, guide me along with those whom
You have guided,
pardon me along with those
whom You
have pardoned,
be an ally to me along with those
whom You are an ally to
and bless for me that which You
have bestowed.
Protect me from the evil You have
decreed,
for verily You decree and none can
decree over You.
For surety, he whom You show allegiance to
is never abased
and he whom You take as an enemy
is never honored and mighty.
O our Lord, Blessed and Exalted are You.

Du'a al Qunoot

And lead us not into temptation but deliver us from evil

Almighty God,
who hast created us in thine own image:
Grant us grace fearlessly
to contend against evil

and to make no peace with oppression;
and, that we may reverently use our freedom,
help us to employ it
in the maintenance of justice
in our communities and among the nations,
to the glory of thy holy Name;
through Jesus Christ our Lord,
who liveth and reigneth with thee
and the Holy Spirit,
one God, now and for ever. Amen.

"Prayer Against Oppression,"
Book of Common Prayer, 1979

Our life is not easy. It is often hard to do what is good. "For I do not do the good I want, but the evil I do not want is what I do" (Rom 7:19). Sometimes it is hard even to know what is good.

AND LEAD US NOT INTO TEMPTATION,
be it hidden or obvious,
sudden or persistent.
BUT DELIVER US FROM EVIL,
past, present or future,
Amen.

St. Francis of Assisi

In all this, in all our life, we cast ourselves on the Lord. Again we come back to the idea of surrender. The theologian Friedrich Schleiermacher went so far as to call religion the "feeling of being ultimately dependent." This led one wag to joke that in that case the dog is the most religious of animals. We live in the midst of dangers—of evil. We ask God to protect us and ultimately to save us from the pitfalls and trials of this world.

And lead us not into temptation.

Q. What does this mean?

A. God tempts no one, of course, but we pray in this request that God will protect us and save us, so that the Devil, the world and our bodily desires will neither deceive us nor seduce us into heresy, despair or other serious shame or vice, and so that we will win and be victorious in the end, even if they attack us.

But set us free from the Evil One.

Q. What does this mean?

A. We pray in this request, as a summary, that our Father in Heaven will save us from every kind of evil that threatens body, soul, property and honor. We pray that when at last our final hour has come, He will grant us a blessed death, and, in His grace, bring us to Himself from this valley of tears.

Martin Luther

For thine is the kingdom and the power and the glory forever and ever. Amen.

This final phrase is not really a part of Jesus' original prayer. It is a doxology which was added in the early Christian church. A doxology is simply a hymn of praise and thanksgiving. For centuries this phrase divided Protestants and Catholics. Catholics would not recite it and Protestants would. This was ironic, for the prayer is Catholic in origin. Today the rift is overcome as Catholics have reincorporated it into the sacred liturgy.

Our Father-Mother God, all harmonious,
Adorable One.
Thy kingdom is come; Thou art ever-present.
Enable us to know; —as in heaven, so on earth, —
God is omnipotent, supreme.
Give us grace for today; feed the famished affections;
And Love is reflected in love;
And God leadeth us not into temptation,
but delivereth us from sin, disease, and death.
For God is infinite, all-power, all Life, Truth, Love, over all, and All.

Science and Health with Key to the Scriptures,
Mary Baker Eddy

Shahadah, Muslim

La ilalha ill-Allah,
Muhammad-ur-rasool ullah.
There is no god but God
and Muhammad is the Messenger of God.

The Shahadah is the first pillar of Islam and is recited many times a day by a Muslim including the five times of daily prayer which make up the second pillar. It is so crucial to Islam that it is printed on the flag of Saudi Arabia.

It is important that you pray this prayer with total conviction—with your whole being. Here we notice a similarity to the Jewish Shema which demands the heart, the soul, and the strength.

When a person of sincerity and sound capacity recites the Shahadah without any mental reservations, he or she fulfills the first requirement for becoming a Muslim. Through this public profession of faith, the individual becomes part of the Islamic community. You then follow up by adopting the other four pillars which make one a good Muslim.

"There is no god but God" means that none has the right to be worshipped but God alone. God does not have a partner. God does not have a son or a father. Associating partners with Allah is called Shirk. Shirk is not only the worship of idols, but also offering prayers or supplications to anyone, living or dead, believing that they hold the same attribute as God. The Qur'an considers Shirk an unpardonable sin.

"You alone do we worship, and You alone do we ask for help."

Surah 1

A Muslim believes in Allah as the Ruler and must not disobey him. In fact everything that exists in the universe obeys him. He is the Fashioner of all the universes that may exist.

"Worship Allah and join no partner with Him."

An-Nisaa 4:36

"Say, He is Allah, the One. The eternally besought by all. He begetteth not, nor was He begotten. And there is no one comparable to Him."

Al-Ikhlas 112:1-4

The Muslim confesses the prophet Muhammad as the servant and Messenger of Allah. This completes one's faith. The Holy Prophet was the greatest of all the prophets of Allah, yet he was only a human being with no share in divinity.

"He who obeys the messengers obeys Allah."

An-Nisaa 4:80

Muhammad is not the only prophet. The Qur'an acknowledges many other prophets, including those of Israel. It also acknowledges Jesus, but does not believe he is God. But Muhammad is the last of the prophets—the most important—since he brings the final revelation, which is Islam with its commands of how to live a godly life.

And We never sent a messenger save with the language of his folk that he might make (the message) clear for them.

Ibrahim 14:4

And there not a nation but a warner has passed among them.

Fatir 35:24

And for every people there is (sent) a guide.

Ar-Ra'd 13:7

The Holy Prophet is the last prophet who brought us the last Book (the Holy Qur'an). "Every prophet before me was sent for his own people but I am sent for all mankind." He lived among his people for a long time and his life is documented in utmost detail. He led his followers by example. The way he lived his life and admonished his followers to live their lives is called the Sunnah of the Holy Prophet.

The second part of the Declaration of Faith makes obeying and following the advice of the prophet Muhammad equally important to the belief in the absolute Unity of Allah. This declaration makes one surrender to the Will of Allah, so one becomes a Muslim—one who completely submits to the will of Allah.

> *So know that Laa ilaaha ill Allah (that there is no deity worthy of worship but Allah), and ask forgiveness for your sin, and also for (the sin of) believing men and believing women. And Allah knows well your moving about, and your place of rest (in your homes).*
>
> Soorah Muhammad (47):19

Serenity Prayer, Christian and Twelve Steps

God give me the serenity
to accept the things I cannot change;
the courage to change the things I can;
and the wisdom to know the difference.

This is the common form of the prayer found today. It is not the original, which is longer and slightly different.

God grant me the serenity
to accept the things I cannot change;
courage to change the things I should;
and wisdom to know the difference.
Living one day at a time;
Enjoying one moment at a time;
Accepting hardships as the pathway to peace;
Taking, as He did, this sinful world
as it is, not as I would have it;
Trusting that He will make all things right
if I surrender to His Will;
That I may be reasonably happy in this life
and supremely happy with Him
Forever in the next.
Amen.

Reinhold Niebuhr

The origins of the Serenity Prayer are something of a mystery. Reinhold Niebuhr is certainly the modern author. It is said that he composed it in 1932 as a tag to a sermon on "Practical Christianity." In 1934 Dr. Howard Robbins asked permission to include the short form in a book of prayers.

Another story suggests Niebuhr attributed the prayer to Friedrich Oetinger, an 18th century theologian. Niebuhr did claim he wasn't sure whether he actually wrote the prayer or remembered it from something he read. Dr. Niebuhr says, "Of course, it may have been spooking around for years, even centuries, but I don't think so. I honestly do believe that I wrote it myself."

In 1939 an early AA member read it in a New York Times obituary column, which read, "Mother—God grant me the serenity to accept things I cannot change, courage to change things I can, and wisdom to know the difference. Goodbye."

He brought the prayer to Bill W., AA's cofounder. The people in AA's office were impressed by the prayer's power and wisdom. "Never had we seen so much AA in so few words," Bill wrote.

The idea of printing the prayer on a small card that could be included in outgoing mail was proposed. Ruth Hock, the Fellowship's first secretary, contacted a member from Washington, D.C., who was a professional printer. The member, Henry S., declined to charge any fee and printed five hundred copies for the group to use.

That's how the simple little prayer became an integral part of the AA movement. "With amazing speed," writes Bill, "the

Crossing all **religious boundaries,** the **Serenity Prayer** may be the **best-loved prayer** in **America.**

Jack Miles

Serenity Prayer came into general use and took its place alongside our two other favorites, the Lord's Prayer and the Prayer of St. Francis."

The U.S.O. followed AA's lead and printed the prayer onto cards to distribute to the troops in World War II, with the permission of Dr. Niebuhr. By then it had also been reprinted by the National Council of Churches. From there the Serenity Prayer has spread throughout the world. It is the one prayer that crosses all boundaries. Although it came out of one tradition, it has found a home in all.

Since this has become a cornerstone of Twelve Step Spirituality, let us explore it as they understand it. We begin with God, which as we have said immediately raises problems for some people. But all that AA asks is that the person begin with the God of their understanding. Of course there is also the expectation that our understanding of God will change and grow over time as we deepen our own spiritual life. But at the very least we are admitting the existence of a power or consciousness greater than our own.

We now ask God for something. By doing so we acknowledge God has the power to do this. We are asking for something that will make us better people. And in doing so we will be of help to others.

We are asking for serenity. That is interesting. We could ask for many other things: patience, love, generosity. Why serenity? We ask for a calm, a peace that will enable us to rise above our ego, to move beyond ourselves.

We realize there are two kinds of problems. There are those over which we can do something. And there are others, like the weather, over which we have no power. It really helps to be able to understand the difference and to let go of what is beyond our will. Accepting this does bring us the beginnings of serenity.

When I live this way I am living in the true present—not in some world of my own dreaming. Acceptance is a key concept of the prayer and something not easily done.

At the beginning of the program, in Step 1, the person admits that he or she is powerless over alcohol and that their life is unmanageable. That demands acceptance that one is an alcoholic. We have to let go of all the lies and excuses that have made up our lives and admit and accept just who we are. But the acceptance does not end there. Acceptance is a state we shall strive for throughout our lives at deeper and deeper levels.

How much sorrow and pain do we create when we fail to realize we cannot change others? We can suggest things to them, but then it is out of our hands and up to them how they receive what we say. Step 12 asks us to take what we have discovered in the program and share it with others. But it cautions us that this is a program of attraction, not promotion. We can only share our own experience and allow the other person to respond as he or she sees fit.

There is a difference here between the prayer as it is found in AA and Niebuhr's original. AA prays for the things that we can change. Niebuhr prays for the things we should change. That "should" adds a deeper dimension.

There are things in our life and in the world that are not just. God asks us to join in the effort to right them. As a spiritual person we come to realize that confronting injustice is our mission. We will not be judged for failing. We will be judged for never trying. The outcome is none of our business. God only asks that we add our hands and voices to the cry of the poor.

We then ask for the courage to change the things we can. We can change our life. And that will demand courage. The spiritual life is not easy. "No one promised us a rose garden." True, there are spiritualities which claim to be easy, but they are false and deceiving.

No transformation is easy. It demands a lot of dying to be born again. AA has some advice for the newcomer: you only have to change two things. First, you have to stop drinking.

Then you have to change your entire life. Harsh, but true. Courage is necessary.

What are the things I can change? They are the things about myself. I cannot change other people. But I can change how I think and how I behave. And that is all I can do.

Finally, we ask for the wisdom to know the difference. Here is the crux of the prayer. Where will we find this wisdom? It is essential so that we can perceive what must be changed and what we should leave alone.

Wisdom is a quality praised in all the spiritual traditions. Often it is equated with God or is portrayed as an emanation of God such as Sophia in the Judeo-Christian tradition. And it is acknowledged to be hard to find. It is not knowledge. It is not technique. It is beyond my limited ego. It is divine. It makes life whole and joyous. In wisdom I become more aware of myself and others and I begin to sense a definite value in loving over being selfish.

Where do we find it? Certainly in the great spiritual traditions. But also from our fellow travelers. Taking my problems to a friend on the journey together we can often see beyond ourselves to the wisdom of God. And above all we receive that wisdom from God which is why we return to this prayer and its simple petitions again and again throughout our lives.

God and Goddess grant me:
The power of Water,
to accept with ease and grace what I cannot change.
The power of Fire,
for the energy and courage to change the things I can.
The power of Air,
for the ability to know the difference.
And the power of Earth,
for the strength to continue my path.

Pagan Serenity Prayer

exploring a great spiritual practice

epilogue

The Words and the Word

At last we come to end of our pilgrimage. We have been near and far. We have visited prayers familiar to us and those unfamiliar. We have remembered prayers from our childhood. And we have read words, words, and words. Although prayer often takes the form of words, there are cautions as well.

Jesus said, "And when you pray, you must not be like the hypocrites; for they love to stand and pray in the synagogues and at the street corners, that they may be seen by men. Truly, I say to you, they have received their reward. But when you pray, go into your room and shut the door and pray to your Father who is in secret; and your Father who sees in secret will reward you. And in praying do not heap up empty phrases as the Gentiles do; for they think that they will be heard for their many words. Do not be like them, for your Father knows what you need before you ask him."

Matthew 6:5-8

We are tempted to look for God in the great events or words. And indeed God may be found there. But God is also found in the small, in what we might be tempted to pass over.

And behold, the Lord passed by, and a great and strong wind rent the mountains, and broke in pieces the rocks before the Lord, but the Lord was not in the wind; and after the wind an earthquake, but the Lord was not in the earthquake; and after the earthquake a fire, but the Lord was not in the fire; and after the fire a still small voice. And when Eli'jah heard it, he wrapped his face in his mantle and went out and stood at the entrance of the cave.

1 Kings 19:11-13

And finally, although we have sought God in all the words of this journey, ultimately God is beyond all words, all attempts to encompass God. That is most truly prayer which lapses into silence.

Be still and know that I am God.

Psalm 46:10

Wa-kon'da,
here needy he stands,
and I am he.

Omaha tribal prayer

The Last Word–Amen

It is traditional in the West to end prayer with the word, "Amen." This practice is common to Jews, Christians, and Muslims. Some have also pointed out its similarity to the Eastern "OM."

It derives from the Hebrew word meaning "So be it." Whenever we say Amen we are affirming and assenting to what has been prayed. It can even become a prayer in itself. By saying Amen you affirm and accept what life God has given you. Let not only your prayer but your entire living, each breath you take, be an Amen.

IX. Amen.

Q. What does this mean?

A. That I should be certain that such prayers are acceptable to the Father in Heaven and will be granted, that He Himself has commanded us to pray in this way and that He promises to answer us. Amen. Amen. This means: Yes, yes it will happen this way.

Martin Luther

AMEN

RICHARD W. CHILSON is a member of the Paulists currently engaged in retreat ministry. His home base is Portland, but he travels widely. He is the author of numerous books, among them *Yeshua of Nazareth: Spiritual Master* , three of the *Thirty Days with a Great Spiritual Teacher* series: *All Will Be Well* (Julian of Norwich), *God Awaits You* (Meister Eckhart), and *You Shall Not Want* (The Psalms), and various titles for Paulist Press, including the best seller *Catholic Christianity: A Guide to the Way, the Truth, and the Life.*